TWELVE EXAMPLES
OF ILLUSION

JAN WESTERHOFF

TWELVE EXAMPLES OF ILLUSION

སྒྱུ་མའི་དཔེ་བཅུ་གཉིས་

OXFORD

UNIVERSITY PRESS

2010

OXFORD
UNIVERSITY PRESS

Oxford University Press, Inc., publishes works that further
Oxford University's objective of excellence
in research, scholarship, and education.

Oxford   New York
Auckland   Cape Town   Dar es Salaam   Hong Kong   Karachi
Kuala Lumpur   Madrid   Melbourne   Mexico City   Nairobi
New Delhi   Shanghai   Taipei   Toronto
With offices in
Argentina   Austria   Brazil   Chile   Czech Republic   France   Greece
Guatemala   Hungary   Italy   Japan   Poland   Portugal   Singapore
South Korea   Switzerland   Thailand   Turkey   Ukraine   Vietnam

Copyright © 2010 Oxford University Press, Inc.

Published by Oxford University Press, Inc.
198 Madison Avenue, New York, NY 10016

www.oup.com

Library of Congress Cataloging-in-Publication Data
Westerhoff, Jan.
Twelve examples of illusion / Jan Westerhoff.
p. cm.
Includes bibliographical references.
ISBN 978-0-19-538735-3
1. Illusion (Philosophy). 2. Buddhist philosophy. I. Title.
B105.I44W47 2010
294.3'42—dc22
2009033100

9 8 7 6 5 4 3 2 1
Printed in China
on acid-free paper

Once upon a time there was a king in India. An astrologer told him: "Whoever shall drink the rain which falls seven days from now shall go mad." So the king covered his well, that none of the water may enter it. All of his subjects, however, drank the water, and went mad, while the king alone remained sane. Now the king could no longer understand what his subjects thought and did, nor could his subjects understand what the king thought and did. All of them shouted "The king is mad, the king is mad." Thus, having no choice, the king drank the water too.

CONTENTS

TWELVE EXAMPLES
OF ILLUSION

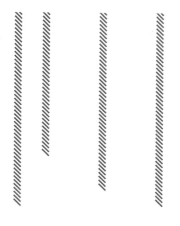

INTRODUCTION

A CERTAIN Tibetan encyclopedia called *A Feast for the Intelligent Mind*[1] lists twelve examples of illusion as follows:

I. Magical illusions

II. The moon in the water

III. Visual distortions

IV. Mirages

V. Dreams

VI. Echoes

VII. A city of Gandharvas

VIII. Optical illusions

IX. Rainbows

X. Lightning

XI. Water bubbles

XII. A reflection in a mirror

The author of this encyclopedia, the eighteenth-century Tibetan scholar Könchog Jigme Wangpo,[2] saw the world as a collection of lists. A well-read and prolific writer like his previous incarnation, he set himself the task of enumerating all the objects that come in pairs, all that come in triples, in sets of four, five, six, or more.

Among other things his encyclopedia tells us about the **two** truths (the absolute and relative truth), the **three** sweet substances (crystalline sugar, sugar-cane juice, and honey), three pursuits of the learned (explanation, debate, and composition), the **four** languages of India (Sanskrit, Prakrit, Apabhraṃśa, and Piśāci[3]), the four kinds of desire between men and women (the desire to gaze upon, the desire to laugh, the desire to hold

---

1. Its full title is མདོ་རྒྱུད་བསྟན་བཅོས་དུ་མ་ནས་འབྱུང་བའི་ཆོས་ཀྱི་རྣམ་གྲངས་ཤེས་ལྡན་ཡིད་ཀྱི་དགའ་སྟོན་ཞེས་བྱ་བ, that is, "An Enumeration of Things Taken from Many Sūtras, Tantras, and Śāstras, called A Feast for the Intelligent Mind."

2. དཀོན་མཆོག་འཇིགས་མེད་དབང་པོ, 1728–1791.

3. Piśāci or Paiśāci is the only language of the four without an extant corpus. The *piśāca* constitute a class of flesh-eating demons, and Piśāci is sometimes regarded as their specific medium of communication. It is more likely, however, that the speakers of Piśāci were actually human, possibly members of an Indian aboriginal tribe regarded as "savages" or "demons."

Könchog Jigme Wangpo

hands, the desire to copulate), the **five** gifts of the cow (urine, dung, milk, butter, curd), the **six** tastes of medicine (sweet, sour, bitter, astringent, hot, and salty), the **seven** parts of an elephant (first leg, second leg, third leg, fourth leg, tail, testicles, trunk), seven constituents of the body (blood, flesh, fat, bone, marrow, semen, and water), the **eight** aspects of water (cool, light, tasty, smooth, clear, without smell, pleasing to the throat, not harmful to the stomach), and the eight grammatical cases (nominative, accusative, instrumental, dative, ablative, genitive, locative, and vocative).

A particularly intriguing piece among the many treasures of this wonder-house of a Tibetan encyclopedia is the list of the twelve examples of illusion. Könchog Jigme Wangpo drew these twelve examples from texts usually classified by Buddhist scholars under the heading "Perfection of Wisdom" or *Prajñāpāramitā* in Sanskrit. The first texts of this sort were probably written in southern India during the first century BCE; their composition continued for the following millenium. They range in length from enormous compendia like the *Perfection of Wisdom in 100,000 Lines* (which amounts to more than a million words of English) to versions that fill a normal-sized volume, such as the *Perfection of Wisdom in 8,000 Lines,* or just a single page, like the famous Heart Sutra, and finally to the ultimately abbreviated recensions in texts like the *Perfection of Wisdom in One Letter,* which consists just of the letter ཨ.

The Perfection of Wisdom texts are notoriously difficult to understand and tend to make the most startling claims. Here is an extract from the *Heart Sutra.*

Matter is emptiness, and emptiness itself is matter. Matter is not distinct from emptiness, and emptiness is not distinct from matter. . . . All things are marked by emptiness, not arisen, not ceased, not pure, not defiled, not diminishing, not increasing. In emptiness . . . there is no eye, no ear, no nose, no tongue, no body, no mind, no shape, no sound, no smell, no taste, nothing to be touched and nothing to be thought of. . . . There is no knowledge, no ignorance, no ending of ignorance, no ending of old age and death, there is no suffering, no cessation of suffering, no path leading to this cessation, there is no wisdom, there is no attainment, and no non-attainment either.

Page showing the list of the twelve examples of illusion (lines 2–3)

Personification of
the Perfection of
Wisdom

Despite their great difficulty and often cryptic style, these texts became so popular that the Perfection of Wisdom was soon personified. Since "Prajñāpāramitā" is a feminine Sanskrit noun, she is depicted in female form. The Tibetan tradition represents her with four arms; the two outer arms hold a book (as befits the personification of wisdom) and a rosary, or sometimes a scepterlike object called a *vajra*, derived from the thunderbolt of the Vedic god Indra and generally regarded as a sign of permanence and indestructibility. Her other two hands are sometimes folded in her lap in the gesture of meditation, holding a vase filled with the nectar of immortality. In the depiction represented here Prajñāpāramitā holds her hands in front of her chest in the gesture of teaching.

The examples of illusion Könchog Jigme Wangpo has collected are only some of those used in the various texts on the Perfection of Wisdom to stress the illusory nature of all phenomena. One of the most famous of them all, the *Diamond Sutra*,[4] concludes with the lines:

---

4. Incidentally, a Chinese translation of this text kept in the British Library is also the oldest printed book bearing a date. It was printed on 11 May 868.

Like stars, like an optical illusion, like a lamp,
like a magical illusion, dewdrops, or a bubble,
like a dream, a flash of lightning or a cloud,
so all that is produced is to be seen.

The optical and magical illusions, the bubble, and the dream also occur in our list; others, like the lamp, the dewdrops, and the cloud, are new. Other texts mention still further examples: an empty fist, an illusory flower appearing in the sky, a shadow, a plantain tree.[5]

Discussing illusions plays such a big role in the Perfection of Wisdom literature because the Buddhist texts state that there is a close connection between the existence of illusion and the existence of suffering. According to the Buddhist worldview, the existence of suffering is neither a necessary feature of the world nor the consequence of a specific fact about the past (such as the fall of Adam), but is rather due to an intellectual error that is mistaken about the way things exist. Suffering is produced by a wrong view of the world, a view that is in fact so much part and parcel of our habitual way of thinking that we are not aware of its perspectival nature any more.[6] More worryingly, the mere intellectual insight into its falsity does not mean that the illusion goes away, in the same way that the mere intellectual insight that the two lines in the diagram below are of the same length does not alter the fact that the lower line *appears* to be longer.

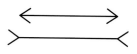

The Müller-Lyer Illusion

As this example shows, an illusion is not something that does not exist, but something that is not what it seems. A cloud that might appear as soft as a white down pillow, as thick as a dark wall, or as far-reaching as the golden sands of the desert when illuminated by the setting sun is really nothing of the sort; in fact it is little more than the thin air into which it will soon disappear.

The aim of the Buddhist enterprise is therefore not just to show that all things are like illusions because the way they appear is different from the way they are. Its aim is to bring about a complete change in how we perceive and

---

5. The plantain tree (*musa paradisiaca*) is in fact an herb with large leaves, the overlapping bases of which form a false trunk. Even though this gives the impression of being a solid stem, it is in fact nothing but a mass of tightly rolled leaves.

6. The philosopher Thomas Metzinger calls such a view of the would "transparent": "A conscious world-model active in the brain is transparent if the brain has no chance of discovering that it is a model—one looks right through it, directly onto the mind, as it were."

conceptualize phenomena. In this way ignorance is cleared away and, one hopes, suffering will completely disappear.

Before getting there, however, it is essential to understand what precisely makes an illusory phenomenon illusory. The twelve examples of illusion listed by Könchog Jigme Wangpo suggest some fascinating examples for addressing this issue and allow us to clarify our ideas about the relation between reality, appearance, perception, deception, and illusion. To their discussion we will now turn.

I shall discuss each example in a separate chapter and will explain what the Indian and Tibetan authors had in mind by using a variety of illustrations from different disciplines, including contemporary philosophy and cognitive science, as well as the history of science, optics, artificial intelligence, geometry, economics, and literary theory. However, I do not expect the reader to have any previous knowledge of any of these and have included a number of pictures and diagrams to make things as clear as possible. Each example throws light on a different aspect of illusion, but the different chapters do not presuppose one another; one can therefore read them in any order. I have tried to keep the text as free as possible from footnotes and technical details. References to all my sources are given at the end of the book; here I also suggest some books suitable for the general reader who wants to learn more about particular topics I discussed.

This book does not come with a conclusion. It is not a textbook on Buddhist philosophy, and I have not tried to defend any particular writer's take on the sources I discuss, not even my own. I encourage the reader to make up her own mind. She will gain most insight by thinking herself about which aspect of illusion each example illustrates, how they all hang together, and which view of the world they support.

MAGIC

 སྒྱུ་མ་

THE TOWN of Śrāvastī, nowadays called Sahet-Mahet, is a thoroughly unremarkable place in northern India where, some not particularly spectacular ruins apart, very little is to be seen.

Nevertheless, two and a half millenia ago some extraordinary events could be witnessed there. This was the time when the Indian prince Siddharta, now, after his enlightenment, known as the Buddha, was staying at Śrāvastī. The gardener of King Prasenajit, a man called Gaṇḍa, had just presented the Buddha with a delicious mango. After eating it the Buddha told Gaṇḍa to plant the seed of the mango fruit. Then

> the Teacher washed his hands over the place where the mango had been planted. The very moment he washed his hands, a mango-tree sprung up, with stalks as thick as a plow-handle, fifty cubits in height. Five great branches shot forth, each fifty cubits in length, four to the four cardinal points and one to the heavens above. Instantly the tree was covered with flowers and fruits; indeed on one side it bore a cluster of ripe mangoes. Approaching from behind, the monks picked the ripe mangoes, ate them, and then withdrew. When the king heard that a mango-tree so wonderful had sprung up, he gave orders that no one should cut it down, and posted a guard. Because the tree had been planted by the gardener Gaṇḍa, it became known as Gaṇḍa's Mango-tree.

This episode is depicted on a stone relief from Bharhut in Madhya Pradesh dating from the third or second century BCE, known as the Ajatashatru pillar. According to the pictorial conventions of the time the Buddha is not shown in human form but represented by an empty throne. Surrounding him are crowds of worshippers admiring the mango tree so wondrously produced.

What is particularly remarkable about this story is the fact that the miracle displayed here by the Buddha, the so-called "mango trick," is a piece of magic

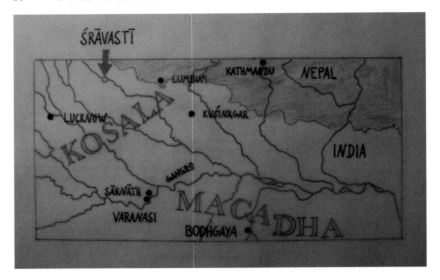

Map showing the location of Śrāvastī

that is still being performed in India. It is one of the most venerable feats of Indian conjuring, second only to the famous (and infamous) Indian rope trick. Here is a description by a German traveler from the first half of the twentieth century; the performance described is not quite as spectacular as the Buddha's feat, but is still impressive.

An apprentice poured a heap of reddish earth, about a foot high, on a piece of cloth in front of the magician. He took the fresh seed of a mango from a not-too-clean bag and showed it to the spectators. Carefully he placed it in the earth, poured some water on it, covered it with a cloth and took a doll from his bag. A whispered conversation with the mysterious thing followed. It was then placed on the cloth and the magician told us in bad English that without the doll the trick could not be performed. After all of this he piped a strange melody on his flute, all the time rocking his emaciated body to and fro. And indeed! Slowly, very slowly the cloth began to move. It rose inch by inch, carrying the doll with it. The Englishman next to me hissed "That's all fake." Three minutes passed. Nobody had touched the cloth. When it was about ten inches high, the apprentice lifted it up. A light-green little mango tree was beneath it! Its long, pointed leaves were still rolled up, but as the magician continued playing his flute they unfolded in front of our eyes. "Oh, how interesting," the Englishman remarked.

Although the Buddha and the anonymous Ceylonese magician perform what is essentially the same trick, there is a noticeable difference in quality. Moreover, the Buddha's performance just gave a taste of the extraordinary show of miracles that was to follow it on that day in Śrāvastī. We read of the Buddha rising into the air, creating a levitating jeweled walk, of flames blazing around his shoulders and water gushing from his feet. All of this is followed by yet another fascinating event.

Relief showing the mango tree miracle (lower section)

> Since the Teacher saw in that vast throng none other than himself who understood his mind and could ask him questions, he put forth his supernatural power and created a double; the double then asked him questions and the Teacher answered them.[7]

The idea of the creation of an illusory person excited the Indian philosophical thinkers to a considerable extent. One particular form of this magical performance is referred to again and again in the Buddhist philosophical literature. Although it sounds quite spectacular, if we are to trust the

---

7. The ability to produce an illusory double of oneself (called *manomaya iddhi* in Pali) as a power supposedly obtained by meditation is already mentioned in the earliest Buddhist writings, such as the *Sāmaññaphalasutta* of the *Dīghanikāya* and the *Mahāsakuludāyisutta* of the *Majjhimanikāya*. For a contemporary scenario involving the creation of virtual voubles see Thomas Metzinger, "The Ego Tunnel", New York, Basic Books, 2009, pp. 98–101.

Magician performing the mango trick

sources one does not have to be a Buddha to bring it about; any ordinary magician will do. Here is what happens.

The conjurer takes some everyday object, such as a piece of wood and shows it to the audience. He then says some mantra or spell, as a result of which the piece of wood appears to the audience as something else: as a chariot, a horse, or an elephant, as a man or as a beautiful woman. The Tibetan philospher Gyal tshab je[8] describes it as follows in a text called *Essence of Good Explanation*:[9]

For instance, the men and women conjured by an illusionist cause the spectators of the magic, who think of them as men and women, to feel attraction and aversion. Though they also appear to the magician, he does not think of them in this way. They do not even appear to those who are unaffected by the spell.

The audience of the magic trick will no longer see the piece of wood but only the beautiful woman and, considering her to be real, will feel attracted to her. The magician himself, interestingly enough, is also under the thrall of his own spells: he does not see a piece of wood either, but the woman

---

8. རྒྱལ་ཚབ་དར་མ་རིན་ཆེན, 1364–1432. Gyal tshab was a famous disciple of Je Tsongkhapa (རྗེ་ཙོང་ཁ་པ), the founder of the Gelug (དགེ་ལུགས) school. Gyal tshab was the first Ganden Tripa (དགའ་ལྡན་ཁྲི་པ) or Holder of the Throne of Ganden. This is the spiritual head of the Gelug school, a position of lesser power than the Dalai Lama but of higher spiritual rank. The Ganden Tripas are appointed and therefore do not constitute a reincarnation lineage. The present Ganden Tripa is the 101st in the succession.

9. The full title of this text is བཞི་བརྒྱ་པའི་རྣམ་བཤད་ལེགས་བཤད་སྙིང་པོ; it is a commentary on Āryadeva's (second to third century) *Four Hundred Verses* (*Catuḥśataka*). The passage in question comments on the twenty-fifth verse of the fifteenth chapter.

Gyal tshab je

as which it appears. Nevertheless he is not completely taken in by the illusion. He *knows* that she is his own creation and can be made to disappear at will. Therefore, one assumes, she does not appear to him quite as attractive (or at least not as attractive in the same way) as to the rest of the audience. The innocent bystanders, finally, who came too late and have not heard the mantra and have therefore failed to be drawn under a spell, see no woman at all. All that appears to them is a crowd of people lecherously eyeing up a piece of wood.[10]

The Tibetans, heavily influenced by Indian culture through the transmission of Buddhism from India, seem to have shared the Indian fascination with illusory persons. They came up with the two related concepts of a *tulku* (སྤྲུལ་སྐུ་) and a *tulpa* (སྤྲུལ་པ་).

"*Tul*" (སྤྲུལ་) means something magically created or an emanation; "*ku*" (སྐུ་) means body. Reincarnations of famous teachers are referred to by the term *tulku*, as are emanations of various figures of the Tibetan pantheon. The Dalai Lama is a *tulku* in both senses, as he is both the incarnation of his respective predecessor and an emanation of Chenrezi (སྤྱན་རས་གཟིགས་), the bodhisattva of compassion. Encountering a *tulku* is not that rare, as there are very many of them around, old and young ones, male and (a few) female ones, some extremely famous and some extremely obscure. Nor is it a particularly mysterious experience, as everybody agrees that apart from their particular spiritual origin *tulkus* are all human beings with human bodies like the rest of us.

Tulpas, on the other hand, are relatively rare (if they exist at all) and are also quite strange phenomena. ("*Pa*" (པ་) is just a nominalizing particle, so *tulpa* can best be translated as "magically created creature.") A *tulpa* is a being that often, but not necessarily, is human in appearance (it might also be an animal, a tree, or suchlike) and that is created purely by someone's mind. A *tulpa* is different from a merely imagined being in that it can be seen *by other people* as well, and in that it may also acquire a certain degree

---

10. We might want to note that this trick could also be performed in reverse. Instead of using a piece of wood to create what is not there, it could also be used to hide what was there. Holding on to such a magically potent stick (called བསྒྲིབ་ཤིང་ in Tibetan), generally taken from the nest of a crow, magpie, or owl, on which *mantras* had been spoken, allowed the bearer to become invisible.

of independence: when the creator wants to dissolve the *tulpa* it might not disappear immediately.

A very detailed report about the creation of a *tulpa* has come down to us. Interestingly, it is not due to a Tibetan, but comes from a French lady, the explorer Alexandra David-Néel. She claims to have spent three years during the 1910s studying at the Kumbum monastery (སྐུ་འབུམ་བྱམས་པ་གླིང་) in Amdo in eastern Tibet.

During her time there, she claims, she created a *tulpa* herself. This she gave the form of a monk, "short and fat, and of an innnocent and jolly type." Shutting herself up in a secluded place she

> proceeded to perform the prescribed concentration of thought and other rites. After a few months the phantom monk was formed. His form grew gradually *fixed* and life-like looking. He became a kind of guest, living in my rooms. I then broke my seclusion and started for a tour, with my servants and tents. The monk included himself in the party. Though I lived in the open, riding on horseback for miles each day, the illusion persisted. I saw the fat *trapa* [གྲ་པ་, a monk] now and then; it was not necessary for me to think of him to make him appear. . . . Once, a herdsman who brought me a present of butter saw the tulpa in my tent and took it for a live lama. . . . [Finally] I decided to dissolve the phantom. I succeeded, but only after six months of hard struggle. My mind-creature was tenacious of life.

Given the many references to the creation of illusory persons by magic both in Buddhist philosophical writings from India and Tibet as well as in other sources such as David-Néel's memoir it is tempting to speculate what, if any, basis in fact this might have. Were there Indian conjurers nearly two thousand years ago capable of performing illusions that would baffle most

Kumbum monastery before its destruction

Alexandra David-Neél at Kumbum

contemporary stage magicians? Was Alexandra David-Néel? And, if so, how did they do it?

We find an interesting description of the technique presumably employed by the Buddha in the creation of his imaginary interlocutor in the *Visuddhimagga*,[11] a voluminous Buddhist commentarial work.

> One who wants to make the mind-made body should emerge from the basic *jhāna* [meditation] and advert to the body in the way already described, and then he should resolve "Let it be hollow." It becomes hollow. Then he adverts to another body inside it, and having done the preliminary work in the way already described, he resolves "Let there be another body inside it." Then he draws it out like a reed from a sheath, like a sword from its scabbard, like a snake from its slough.

Although this description will presumably not enable us to try this out at home immediately, it deals with the creation of illusory bodies in a refreshingly matter-of-fact way. In this respect it is quite unlike attempts at theorizing we find in some modern writers such as W.Y. Evans-Wentz, chiefly known nowadays for bringing out the first translation of the *Bardo Thodöl* (བར་དོ་ཐོས་གྲོལ་, the *Tibetan Book of the Dead*). According to him the trick is "changing the body's rate of vibration," inhibiting the "emanation of its radioactivity," or, alternatively, "exuding ectoplasm."

---

11. Its author, Buddhaghosa, lived in the fifth century.

A somewhat more intelligible (if not particularly convincing) account sometimes put forward to explain a variety of Indian magical performances (such as the rope trick[12] and the mango trick) describes them as the effect of mass hypnosis. Unfortunately this is little more than a redescription of the effect, since most information about this phenomenon seems to be anecdotal. We have very little hard evidence of examples of mass hypnosis of this kind, nor any convincing theories of how it may work.

But regardless of whether or not we credit the ancient Indian and Tibetan magicians with performing the illusionistic feats ascribed to them in the philosophical texts, their magical tricks remain a fascinating example of illusion. This is because a magician who can bring about performances very much like them is very close by. It is our own mind.

Let us look at two remarkable examples. The first consists of creating an illusory appearance of something that is really not there. Have a look at the figure below.

What you see here is a faintly glowing worm with blue stripes in front of a series of black stripes. The amazing thing about this figure is that you see a blue hue even between the blue stripes, while in fact *there is no blue color there*. If you direct a photometer at this part of the page you will see that no color is reflected. You can also easily convince yourself by covering two of the blue stripes with a piece of paper while looking at the space in between: it will appear as pure white. As with any good illusion *knowing* this makes no difference at all. What you know you should see does not affect what you actually see.

If the blue color you see is not caused by blue color on the page, it must be caused by something else. It is something created by the illusionistic powers of your mind that constructs a blue worm from a series of blue stripes. But why do our minds create such illusions? Usually when we perceive "bitty" things like the collection of blue lines there is in fact a single object causing them, not a collection of disconnected parts. For example, a snake seen through the foliage of a tree or through a network of shadows could appear in such a way that only parts of it are visible. Conceptualizing this quickly as

Appearance of the non-existent

---

12. An account of the rope trick that ascribes it to mass hypnosis (or "mesmerism," as the author calls it) can be found in T. Secrett's *Twenty-five Years with Earl Haig* (London: Jarrolds, 1929), pp. 43–60.

a single object obviously has evolutionary advantages, which explains why we ended up with a visual system that, like a conjurer, sometimes shows us more than there is to see.

Interestingly enough, we can create the very same effect with sounds. Suppose I play a continuous sound, say, A♭, immediately succeeded by some white noise, which is in turn immediately succeeded by A♭. What you hear is not such a sequence of three distinct auditory events, but you hear A♭ all the time, first on its own, then against the white noise, then on its own again. In fact, such sequences of overlaid sounds are far more common (and therefore interpreted by your auditory system as far more likely) than artificially created ones where one sound starts at exactly the same moment when another sound stops. (In fact the illusion of the continuous tone can be avoided by inserting a very small gap between the end of the A♭ and the beginning of the white noise.) Again, it is clear why a cognitive system that creates such illusions is eminently successful in a world like ours. There are many overlying objects and overlaid tones, but only few fragmentary ones.

Now let us consider a case that looks like the disappearance of something that really *is* there. No magical stick will be required for this performance. Look at two symbols below, a star and a circle. Hold the page about eighteen inches in front of you and close your right eye. Look straight at the circle, now slowly move the page toward your face, making sure all the time that your vision is fixed on the circle. About halfway the star on the left will disappear. What you see is a page with only one symbol, namely the circle. The star will have vanished.

At one level the explanation of this phenomenon is very simple. The retina of the eye is covered with photoreceptive cells, apart from an area of about one-sixteenth of an inch in diameter where it is connected to the optical nerve. This so-called blind spot is located about fifteen degrees away from the fovea, the area of sharpest vision, and covers about six degrees of visual angle. This means that about a foot away a postage stamp could vanish in the blind spot, as could a person's head when it is twelve feet away.

Where there are no photoreceptive cells we are obviously unable to see anything. What happens as you move the diagram closer to your face is that the light reflected from the black star finally falls on the blind spot and is therefore not registered by your visual system. An interesting question

 ●

Disappearance of the existent

arises once we ask what we see where we don't see anything, that is, what we see at the place of the blind spot. Our visual field does not seem to have any gaps or blanked-out parts (like a TV screen with a Post-it note stuck to it) but is continuous. We realize that when the black star disappears, we see a blank page in its place, not a blank page with gaping hole. The area where we see nothing appears to us just like the surrounding bits of our visual space.

It therefore becomes apparent that the illusion created by the mind is not the disappearance of the black star—this is simply due to the structure of the retina and is in itself no more surprising than that we cannot taste any-thing by holding it in our hand, as there are no taste buds on our fingertips. The illusion is that we see something else in its place that is not there in reality: the piece of paper covered by our blind spot is not white, but shows a black, star-shaped figure. We are therefore all suffering from partial visual anosognosia, or Anton's syndrome. This term is used to describe the curi-ous case of blind patients who nevertheless claim they can see. Because they obviously have difficulties getting around in daily life, they invent the most ingenious explanations, apart from the one obvious one, namely that they are blind.[13] While Anton's symptoms might justifiably strike us as a some-what bizarre psychological condition, we should note that on a small scale our minds are playing exactly the same trick on us. We are not even aware that there are parts of our visual field with which we cannot see and that the continuity of our field of vision is a mere illusion.

Having considered the abilities of our own mind to let us see things that are not there, and to make things that are there disappear, the magic tricks described in the beginning of the chapter may no longer appear so spectacular. The production of an illusory mango tree or an illusory woman is admittedly a bit more intricate than the production of an illusory blue hue, but there seems to be no fundamental difference in kind. Similarly, making the star on the page invisible or making a man invisible is a difference in complexity, not a difference in the sort of illusion produced.

Of course I do not want to claim that the magic tricks described could be completely explained by reference to phenomena like the filling in of blue color or the blind spot. But the important point to note is that the *kinds* of illusion represented by the examples discussed, which make them interesting

---

13. It is interesting to note that the reverse of this condition (seeing people who claim to be blind) exists as well. If these patients are asked to *guess* the kind of pattern presented to them (which they deny being able to see) they guess correctly well over 90 percent of the time.

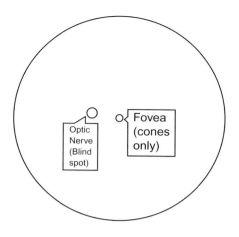

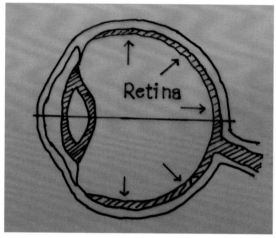

The blind spot

examples of illusion, are not very different from the illusions that form an integral part of our everyday perception of the world.

We might object that the visual illusions described are in fact very rare and isolated cases. We need to construct a picture carefully in order to produce the ghostly blue color. Furthermore, things do not disappear regularly in our blind spot: having two eyes generally takes care of this. Leaving aside these particular cases, our perception of the world, it may be argued, is therefore more or less the way the world is. In most cases we are more like people watching a real elephant, rather than a merely illusory one.

In reply I would like to discuss something that is sometimes called the *grand illusion* of consciousness. This is our firm conviction that consciousness is continuous. What do we mean by this? In the first place we think that our visual field is continuous. Visual perception is like seeing an internal movie: every part of our mental screen is filled in, there are no gaps or interruptions. But apart from this assumption of the spatial continuity of the visual field, we also feel that our consciousness is temporally continuous (apart from times when we are asleep or unconscious). One scene in our internal movie follows the next, and if we close our eyes, still images, sounds, feelings, smells, and thoughts follow one another in quick succession without any apparent gap.

All of this seems so obvious that it is hardly worth stating. Even more absurd seems the attempt to question it. After all, what could we be more sure about than the way our own consciousness is structured? How could we possibly be mistaken about this?

Yet I want to argue that the spatial and temporal continuity of our consciousness is an illusion, a magic trick played by our own mind. Because it is so fundamental it makes sense to call it the grand illusion, but it is an illusion nevertheless.

It is tempting to infer from the "screenlike" nature of the retina that there must also be some mental screen on which the mental image is projected. But even the retina is at best a screen with a hole in it (the blind spot), a fact that is only compensated for to some extent by the fact that there are two of them. To see that the retina is really not like a projective screen displaying a uniform and focused picture from the center to the boundaries, consider the following simple experiment that you can try at home. Take a pack of cards and mix them. Take out one card but don't look at it. Fixate your eyes on some object straight in front of you, then take up the card with an outstretched arm (with its face towards you) and slowly move your stretched arm toward the point you are fixating. Try to identify where your arm is when you finally notice what kind of card you picked.

It is instructive to try this experiment in your mind first. One generally thinks that it should be possible to know what the card is fairly quickly, perhaps when the arm is at thirty or perhaps forty-five degrees. But the astonishing fact is that you will not be able to tell what kind of card you are looking at until the card is exactly in your focal area (that is, the point straight in front of you which you have been fixating).

The fovea, located two to three degrees from the center of the retina, has a resolution that is about ten times higher than the rest of the retina. It is this area of the retina that the image of the playing card has to fall on in order to be fully discriminated. The reason why our visual field does not appear to us that way (in other words, as clear and focused in the dead center, but blurred and fuzzy elsewhere) is because our eyes are not stationary but are continously moving, tracking an object or jumping around in shifty movements called *saccades*.

We might find it astonishing (and perhaps even shocking) to realize how much discontinuity in our visual field we do not even notice. It is not that we ignore the gap created by our blind spot or overlay it with information from our other eye—even when looking with one eye we quite literally see nothing missing. When an object is projected onto the blind spot it just seems to disappear behind a magic screen. Similarly, we do not realize that our eyes are continuously shifting here and there, even when we think we are observing something with a steady gaze. It seems as if we are taking in all of a visual scene at once, but in fact our eyes are constantly switching between its different parts.

The temporal continuity of our consciousness during our waking life seems to rest on an equally shaky foundation. A relatively well-known phenomenon that should cause us to raise some doubts is the so-called time-gap experience familiar to motorists. This usually happens when driving on a familiar route. We suddenly "wake up" and realize that we have no recollection of the immediately preceding time. It appears as if the last half an hour or so is just missing from our lives.

We obviously had been able to react to quite complex stimuli while driving, such as working steering, brakes, and gears, keeping the car on the road, reacting to traffic-lights, and avoiding crossing pedestrians. To this extent we hardly want to say that we were unconscious during the "missing time," at least not in the way we say of a sleeping or comatose person that they are unconscious. On the other hand we do not have any memory of completing these complex actions and we hardly want to assume that we somehow suddenly forgot about all this before "waking up."

The time-gap experience is only one of the more extreme cases of the temporal discontinuity of consciousness; in fact shorter experiences of a similar sort happen frequently when we carry out familiar and habitual tasks, such as walking, reading, or writing. We usually do not notice the accompanying gaps in consciousness, but to conclude from this that there is in fact a continuous flow of consciousness is just like inferring that there is a light continuously on in your fridge, just because it is always on whenever you happen to check.

Considering these arguments it appears the cognitive illusions we are prone to are not just rare and isolated effects resulting from looking at carefully constructed diagrams or from performing visual machinations with one eye closed. There is an illusion at the very center of our life. Our consciousness, something that we all *seem* to know is a continous, smoothly flowing structure without holes or gaps, is in fact nothing like this. Our consciousness is discontinuous in the extreme, although it does not appear to us to be so. Taking this into account it seems perhaps a little less counterintuitive when the Buddha says that "consciousness is a magic show, a juggler's trick entire." This might be exactly what consciousness is.

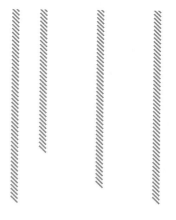

THE MOON
IN THE WATER

ཚ་ཟླ་

NEXT TO the entrance of most Tibetan temples one finds a mural showing the Wheel of Life,[14] a diagrammatic representation of the different places one can be reborn in—as a god, a human, an animal, in hell, and so forth. The Wheel is held in the clutches of a fierce demonic figure; this is Yama,[15] the lord of death. Yama's holding the wheel indicates that beings everywhere, even those reborn in the realms of the gods, must die, to be reborn again and again, countless times. At the top of some pictures of the Wheel of Life we see the Buddha standing on a bank of clouds, pointing at the full moon.

Sometimes the moon is accompanied by a short inscription saying that the Buddha makes us move toward his teaching. The goal of these teachings, liberation from the circular succession of birth and death, is represented by the moon emerging from behind the clouds.

The full moon, a highly auspicious symbol in all Asian cultures, is intricately connected with the Buddha's life: his birth, enlightenment, first teaching, and his death are all said to have occurred on full moon days and are celebrated accordingly following the lunar calendar used by most Buddhist countries. The moon pervades Tibetan culture in many respects: moon disks resting on lotus flowers provide the support of deities of the Tibetan pantheon, are held as attributes or adorn the top of reliquary monuments.[16]

But as soon as we do not deal with the moon itself, but with its reflection in the water, its interpretation changes from a symbol of enlightenment and liberation to an example of illusion. This is nicely illustrated by the well-known Tibetan tale of the monkeys and the moon.

---

14. སྲིད་པའི་འཁོར་ལོ་
15. གཤིན་རྗེ་
16. མཆོད་རྟེན་

The Wheel of Life

At one time a band of monkeys saw the reflection of the moon in a lake and thought there was a second moon swimming in the lake. Immediately they decided to get hold of the silvery shining disk. They all climbed on a tree with branches overhanging the lake. The head monkey decided that they should form a chain: he would go first, someone holding him by his tail, then another monkey would grab the second monkey's tail, continuing in this way

Buddha pointing out the Moon

Standing Avalokiteśhara (detail)

Top of a Stūpa

Candra (detail)

until he reached the surface of the lake. They set out to do this, but when the chain was halfway down to the water the branch broke and all the monkeys fell into the lake. Their big splash rippled the still surface of the lake and the reflected moon disappeared.

This cautionary tale warns us against mistaking the reflection of some object for the thing itself, thereby grasping at an object that is not there. A commentary on the Perfection of Wisdom sutras ascribed to the second-century Buddhist philosopher Nāgārjuna called *The Great Treatise on the Perfection of Wisdom* informs us that

> when a small child sees the moon reflected in the water it happily wants to reach out for it, but adults which see this laugh at him. In the same way an ignorant one, considering his body, thinks that he has a self. . . . It is in the still water that one sees the reflection of the moon, but once one stirs up the water, the reflection disappears. Similarly in the still water of an ignorant mind one finds the conception "this is me." But when the stick of wisdom has troubled the water of thought one sees the self no longer.

Monkey Reaching for the Moon

Here the illusory appearance of the moon in the water is used as an illustration of the Buddhist view that the self is an illusory appearance too. While we have the strong impression that there is something distinct from our bodies, sensations, thoughts, feelings, memories, and so forth that is "me," the Buddhist wants to argue that there is no such thing. We superimpose the notion of a self on the rapidly changing complex of bodily and mental events, but this

The child Krishna
Reaching for the
Moon in a Puddle

superimposition is nothing but a convenient mental construction, nothing
that exists as a matter of fact.

It is easy to misunderstand this use of the example of the moon in the
water. While the reflection of the moon is obviously not the moon, there
is something causing that reflection: the real moon in the sky. We might
think that similarly even though the self is not to be found in our body,
thoughts, feelings, and so forth, the real "me" does exist, but not where we
think it is. This, however, is very different from the Buddhist view and is
more in accordance with the system of Advaita Vedānta as taught by the
eight-century Indian philosopher Śaṅkara. According to the Buddhist interpretation there is no real "me," no absolute, inaccessible self hidden behind
a mistaken superimposition.

A better illustration of the Buddhist view of the self that does not give rise to such misunderstandings is provided by the images we see in the moon. Different people at different times have seen different things in the moon, such as a man, a woman, and a jumping cow (see illustrations on the next page).

The cow here has to be seen as jumping to the left, its head hidden at the dark side of the moon. The Tibetans (like many other Asians) see the image of a rabbit in the moon.[17] Sometimes this animal is depicted as a usual, sitting hare, as in the painting reproduced at the beginning of this chapter; sometimes the rabbit stands up and uses a pestle to compound the nectar of immortality.[18] (See illustrations on page 30.)

Of course there is no image of anything in the moon, neither man, nor woman, nor cow, nor rabbit, nor anything else. All of these diverse images are the product of a psychological condition called *pareidolia*. Pareidolia is the superimposition of a pattern on something that is patternless, such as blobs of ink on a page, clouds, or the marks on the surface of the moon. Our minds project an image onto the collection of the dark spots on the moon, thereby creating something that does not exist. Our ability to see faces in many essentially random arrangements of marks is very likely hardwired in our brains. Animals with such an ability have a clear evolutionary advantage. For newborn infants it is useful to be able to react quickly to the mother's face, while in later life the ability to recognize swiflty different facial expressions is essential in social interaction.

According to the Buddhist view, our conception of the self is an illusory projection of the same quality as the projection of images onto the moon. Onto the basis of a changing and ephemeral collection of physical and psychological events we project the notion of a permanent self underlying our bodies, our thoughts, feelings, desires, and beliefs. Their relation to this self is what makes our bodies *our* bodies, our thoughts *our* thoughts, and so forth. It is tempting to assume an evolutionary explanation for this conception of the self as well. Using this notion of a self we are able to unify our diverse sensory perceptions, to establish the boundaries of our bodies (so that we do

---

17. Seeing a rabbit in the moon might be made easier by one's point of observation. At the more southerly latitudes at which many Asian countries are located, the moon has a lower angle of inclination so that the face is "turned" by up to about ninety degrees. If the reader tries turning an image of the moon in a similar way she will realize that the rabbit becomes easier to see.

18. The Japanese see it, more profanely, as making rice cakes. Interestingly enough the Japanese terms for the full moon (望月, mochizuki) and for the production of rice cakes (餅つき, mochitsuki) are phonetically very similar.

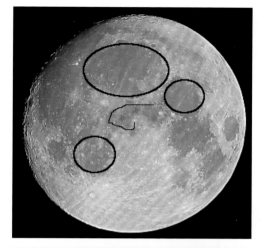

Man in the moon

Woman in the moon

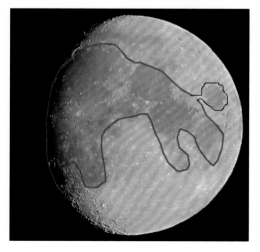

Cow in the moon

Images of the rabbit in the moon

not devour ourselves), to establish how tall we are, how fast we can run, and so forth. All of this is of eminent importance for survival. Nevertheless, the Buddhist will want to argue that, apart from its pragmatic use, there is no self, in the same way as there is no image in the moon apart from the mythological, narrative, or aesthetic uses the projection of such images might have. It is by assuming that such a self is real that suffering is produced. By realizing the absence of the self, like seeing the moon empty of images, we obtain liberation and freedom from suffering.

The projection of images onto the moon is not just confined to the history of mythology or folklore. It also occurs in early modern astronomy. The example I have in mind here is the mysterious case of Galileo's "Bohemian" crater on the moon. Reporting what he saw on the moon through his telescope Galileo wrote in the *Starry Messenger, Revealing Great, Unusual and Remarkable Spectacles . . . With the Aid of a Spyglass Lately Invented*:

> There is another thing which I must not omit, for I beheld it not without a certain wonder; this is that almost in the center of the moon there is a cavity larger than all the rest, and perfectly round in shape. I have observed it near both first and last quarters, and have tried to represent it as correctly as possible in the second of the above figures. As to light and shade, it offers the same appearance as would a region like Bohemia if that were enclosed on all sides by very lofty mountains arranged exactly in a circle. Indeed, this area on the moon is surrounded by such enormous peaks that the bounding edge adjacent to the dark portion of the moon is seen to be bathed in sunlight before the boundary of light and shadow reaches halfway across the same space.

In the illustration on the next page the crater can be clearly made out on the dividing line between light and shadow. The curious fact now is that the Bohemian crater does not exist. As a quick look at a photograph of the moon will confirm, there is nothing like a crater of this size at the location indicated. Given that Galileo was an astronomical observer of extraordinary skill, one does wonder where the illusory crater came from. An obvious explanation would be to blame it on imperfections of the "spyglass," or Galilean telescope. As a tool for astronomic investigations it is known to have produced a whole range of visual illusions, from variations of the placement of the image seen to the mysterious doubling of observed objects. But even if the Bohemian crater was an illusion created by the telescope Galileo used, the difficulty remains that the crater would actually be large enough

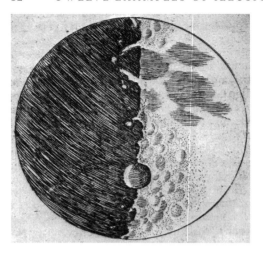

The Bohemian crater

to be seen with the naked eye. (You can easily try this out for yourself by propping up the book and looking at Galileo's picture of the moon from about five yards away to simulate the apparent size of the moon. The crater is quite small but still visible.) Galileo, as well as everybody else, could just have looked up at the moon with unaided vision in order to see quite clearly that there was no Bohemian crater.

So why did he still believe in the description of such a crater? There are at least two different but equally interesting theories. According to the first, the Bohemian crater is a product of seeing what you believe, rather than of believing what you see. This is to say that once Galileo had come up with the belief that there was such a crater (perhaps due to shortcomings of the telescope) he then superimposed what he believed he saw onto the information coming in through his eyes. Such a crater would have been useful evidence in support of Galileo's argument that the moon, having valleys and mountains, was in many respects quite like the earth, rather than a perfectly smooth celestial body of a very different nature. Because he held on to the important belief that there was such a crater, for Galileo at least there was no difference in what he saw through the telescope and what he saw by the naked eye: the Bohemian crater featured in both.

Evidence for the extent to which our expectations influence what we see can be found in the famous "anomalous playing-card experiment." In this experiment the subjects were shown a playing card, such as the five of spades, the ace of hearts, and so on, for short intervals (less than a second) and had to identify the card they saw. Some of the cards, however, were doctored: for example, there was a black three of hearts or a red two of spades. What the subjects usually reported when shown these cards was not what the card presented to them displayed, but a "normalized" version coherent with their expectations. A red four of spades would thus be described as either a red four of *hearts* (thus changing the form) or as a *black* four of spades (changing the color). As the subjects did not believe that there were

  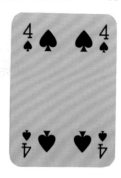

When this is shown   This is seen   Or this

going to be any anomalous cards shown to them, their observations were changed accordingly. Rather than believing what they saw, they saw what they believed they would see.

The second interpretation of Galileo's observation of the nonexistent crater was for some time adopted by the philosopher of science Paul Feyerabend (though he later regarded it as less plausible). It says that *we do not see the same thing* when we look at the moon with the naked eye that people during Galileo's time saw. Our perception of the moon's surface is more distinct and definite than theirs was, due to the practice of telescopic observation and exposure to images of the moon, while the perception of our ancestors was more hazy and indistinct.

This idea was suggested to Feyerabend by considering a multitude of theories about the moon from classical antiquity that apparently contradict what we can all see with the naked eye. The Greek astronomer and philosopher Anaximander (ca. 610–ca. 547 BCE), for example, assumed that the earth was surrounded by rings of fire encapsulated in opaque air. These rings were only visible in the parts where the air had little slits or vents through which the fire inside could be seen. The stars were therefore no celestial objects, but tiny apertures allowing us to look into the fire hidden inside the rings. The same was true of the moon, though this aperture opened and closed regularly, thereby generating the phases of the moon.

But this account seems to be in obvious contradiction with what we can observe with the naked eye: if the moon was a moving aperture it should not show the kind of constant face we observe it to have. Assuming that the natural philosophers of antiquity were just as sharp as we are it becomes hard to understand why they should have adopted such wildly implausible theories—that is, unless we assume that what they saw when they looked at

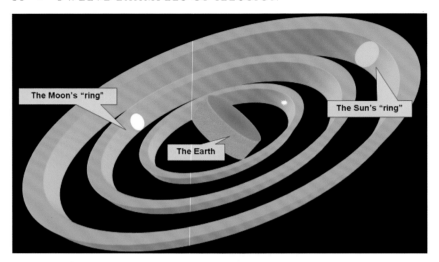

Anaximander's view of the universe

the moon is significantly different from what we see. The second interpreta-tion thus assumes that not just our interpretations, but also our observations are time dependent. Not only can how we interpret what we see can change with history (a claim few would dispute in any case)—what we see in the very same object may change as well.

This second interpretation is of course a lot more far-reaching (and, some might argue, a lot less credible) than the first. But even using the first inter-pretation we realize the force of our *assumptions* about what we see in shap-ing what we actually see. The force of superimposition does not just allow the viewer to read images of animals into patterns of an essentially random nature, it can also project images without any apparent foundation at all, as in the case of the Bohemian crater.

Our account of the illusions of the moon would not be complete without mentioning the most famous of all of them, so famous in fact that it is often just referred to as *the* moon illusion. This illusion is the puzzling fact that the full moon appears to us significantly larger when it is seen close to the hori-zon than when it is up high in the sky. Reports of this phenomenon go back to very early times—it is already described by the Chinese philosopher Lieh Yü-k'ou (列禦寇) (fourth century BCE). A puzzling fact about the moon illu-sion itself is that there is still no theoretical consensus about how to explain it. A long series of papers and, most recently, a book of nearly three hundred pages have been written about it, so there is no lack of theories purporting to explain it. However, the theories different writers propose vary widely, and at the moment it does not look as if any one of them is likely to win acceptance by the majority. One reason for this is that any possible explanation has to address problems from fields as diverse as astronomy, mathematics, psychology, and philosophy, so that the number of issues one can disagree about and the number of mistakes one can make is greatly increased.

At least there is some agreement about the explanations that do not work at all. The moon, being a solid celestial body, obviously does not actually change in size. So it is not the moon's real size that changes, but its apparent size. The term "apparent size," however, can mean a number of different things. If you take a coin from your pocket, hold it close to your eyes, and then stretch out your arm to look at it from a greater distance, the apparent size of the coin changes. The coin does not get any smaller as you move it away from your eyes, but the image of the coin projected onto your retina gets smaller. So we could agree that by the term "apparent size" we mean the size of the object's image at the back of your eyes. Now how could this explain the moon illusion? It cannot be a simple perspectival phenomenon as in the case of the coin, because the moon close to the horizon and the moon high up in the sky are the very same distance from your eyes.[19] But for the retinal image to get smaller, the moon seen high up would have to be further away.

Another possible cause of a change in the size of the retinal image that does not require the object to move is atmospheric refraction. The Greek astronomer Ptolemy (second century CE) in his *Almagest* was the first to offer this as an explanation of the moon illusion, arguing that it was due to "the moist atmosphere surrounding the earth," which got between the celestial bodies and our sight. Now it is in fact true that the paths of light rays change when they enter a different medium, such as when they go from air to water (which is why an immersed stick looks bent) or from the near vacuum of outer space to the atmosphere of the earth. But unfortunately this change in the direction of light rays, also known as *refraction*, cannot explain the moon illusion. As the moon approaches the horizon, more and more atmosphere gets in between it and our eyes. This affects the light rays coming from it: the image of the moon will look vertically squashed and its color will assume a slightly reddish tint.

---

19. This is not exactly true. Because we have to take the earth's radius into account, the moon just over the horizon is about 2 percent *farther away* than when it is up in the sky. According to the perspectival theory the moon at the horizon should therefore appear a little bit smaller than when it is up in the sky, rather than considerably larger.

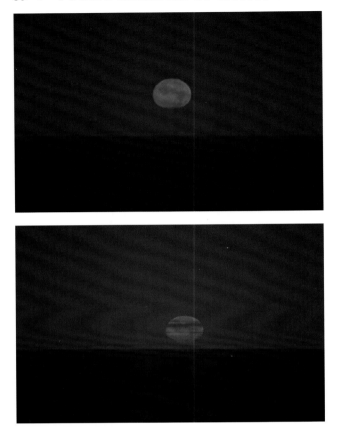

Effects of refraction on the moon

However, the horizontal width of the moon will remain unaffected. So Ptolemy's account cannot really tell us why the moon as a whole looks larger at the horizon; it just explains why it looks slightly deformed.

The difficulty with both the perspectival account as well as Ptolemy's theory based on atmospheric refraction is that they are based on understanding the apparent size of the moon as the size of the image on our retinas. But in fact the size of the retinal image does not change at all as the moon moves across the sky. You can easily test this for yourself with three matches. If you hold them next to one another at arm's length they will fully cover the moon high up in the sky. They will also cover it when it is close to the horizon. However, if the horizon moon's retinal image was larger than the sky moon's it should extend beyond the width of the matches.

The horizontal width of the moon is about half a degree of visual angle no matter where it is in the sky. This explains why the moon illusion does not show up on photographs. If we photograph the moon at different positions in the sky and then superimpose the two spheres, their sizes will exactly match. Yet the fact remains that the moon close to the horizon will appear to be about one-and-a-half times larger than its horizontal width of half a degree. We therefore have to conclude that we cannot spell out the apparent size of the moon in terms of the size of the image at the back of our eyes. The moon illusion, and this is a point virtually all writers agree on, is not an optical but a psychological illusion. When we speak of the moon's "apparent size," we must mean the size ascribed to it in our mental representation.

Among the various psychological explanations of the moon illusion two are particularly interesting. The first assumes that the moon illusion is a manifestation of the same effect we also find in the well-known Ebbinghaus illusion.

The circles at the center of the two figures below are the same size. Yet the one on the left seems considerably larger than the one on the right. This is because both central circles are not observed in isolation but in the context of their surroundings. Relative to the small circles surrounding it the circle on the left looks big, while the circle on the right is dwarfed by its enormous neighbors.

It is apparent that the moon at the horizon is usually seen against the contrast of objects that occupy a smaller portion of visual space than the half degree covered by the disk of the moon, such as shrubs, trees, or houses seen from afar, or even the distance between the moon and the horizon (although this is not an object in the same sense as a barn or a house, it fulfills a similar role in perception). When it is high up in the sky, on the other hand, the objects surrounding the moon, such as clouds, the gaps between them, or

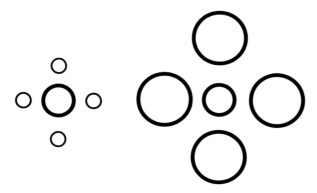

Ebbinghaus illusion

even the vast, relatively empty expanse of the zenith sky, occupy a significantly larger visual area than that of the moon itself. For this reason the moon appears smaller against this contrast of large objects than it does against the contrast of small objects when it is close to the horizon.

While this explanation does seem quite plausible it fails to account for another puzzling feature of the moon illusion. If one turns around, bends forward, and then looks at the moon near the horizon through one's legs it suddenly looks significantly smaller. Yet the relations of contrast with its surroundings have remained the same: an upside-down house at the horizon still occupies the same amount of visual space, so that the apparent size of the moon should not be affected.

The second psychological explanation regards the moon illusion as an example of another popular optical illusion, the Ponzo illusion.

As can be easily checked with a ruler, the two white bars superimposed on the railroad tracks are the same size. Yet the one higher up appears to be larger. This is essentially because we do not regard it as "higher up" but as "farther away": we do not see the drawing as a flat piece of paper but as a perspectival representation of three-dimensional space with depth. The bars, which are part of this representation, are therefore seen to be objects located along the length of the railroad track. By *assuming* that the upper

Ponzo illusion

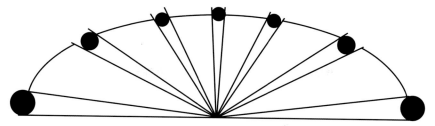

Sky-dome model

bar is farther away we also have to think that the object it represents is considerably larger than the one represented by the lower bar, for only in this case it could produce a retinal image of the same size as the lower one. If the objects represented by the two bars were the same size, the upper one should occupy less retinal space, because it is further away. Since it does not do so we consider it to be larger, and this is how it appears to us in perception.

In order to see how all of this applies to the moon illusion we have to take into account the mental model we have of the sky. Compare the apparent difference between the perceived distance across to an unobstructed horizon (for example when standing on a boat in the middle of the ocean) and the distance up toward the clouds. Most people will say that the distance to the horizon appears greater. In this example the horizon will be about three miles away. Altocumulus clouds, which are located at mid-level between the low stratus and the high cirrus clouds, can be more than three-and-a-half miles up. Despite the fact that these distances are nearly the same it still looks to us as if the dome of the sky is significantly less high than it is long or wide. The mental model we apply to the sky is a soup bowl turned upside-down.

If we now project the moon onto the interior of this soup bowl it becomes apparent that we must regard the moon at the horizon to be farther away than the moon high up in the sky, in the same way in which we regard the upper bar in the Ponzo illusion to be farther away than the lower one. But given that the moon produces retinal images of the same size no matter where it is in the sky, we conceive of the horizon moon as larger, to compensate for the farther distance away we assume it to be. On this interpretation the moon illusion is an illusion because it is based on a faulty mental model. The heavens do not have the shape of an inverted soup bowl, even though this shape seems to suggest itself to us naturally. From this model we draw the mistaken assumption that the horizon moon is further away from us, which, together with the correct assumption that things that are farther away look smaller, makes us think that the moon at the horizon must be larger than the moon high up in the sky in order to produce an image the same size at the back of our eyes. Hence the illusory appearance of difference in size.

Looking at different illusory phenomena connected with the moon has shown us something about the dependence of what we perceive on our beliefs and assumptions. We only see an image of a cow or a rabbit on the face of the moon if we know what we are looking for. The belief that there is such an image allows us to project it onto an essentially random collection of spots. In the case of the Bohemian crater, Galileo's belief in its existence even let him superimpose a faulty impression produced by his telescope onto what he saw with the naked eye. Here, as in many other cases described in the psychological literature, it was not that perceptions brought us beliefs about what we perceived, it was rather the beliefs bringing us perceptions of what we believed. As the soup bowl analysis of the moon illusion showed, such beliefs do not have to be explicit. Few would go around asserting that the heavens are shaped like an inverted bowl, yet this apparently natural assumption has important implications for how we perceive celestial objects.

It therefore seems very apt that Buddhist writers used the illusions of the moon as an illustration of the illusory projected self. For it seems to us plainly evident that we, as persons, have permanent or at least very stable selves distinct from our bodies and the things going on in our minds. That there is a self that is the owner of our bodies, the experiencer of our mental lives, and the agent of our actions appears as obvious as something we can clearly see in front of us. But, as we have just seen, what we can clearly see in front of us is sometimes just the product of the *belief* about what is there in front of us, and not a reflection of what is really there.

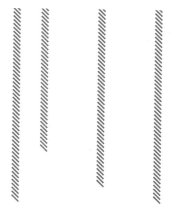

A VISUAL DISTORTION

མིག་ཡོར་

IN ONE of his major philosophical treatises, a long work called *The Introduction to the Middle Way*, the seventh-century Indian philosopher Candrakīrti describes the following example of a visual distortions:

> Suppose that a man suffering from a visual distortion is holding a white vase in his hand, and caused by this distortion he sees what appear to be strands of hair on the surface of the vase. He wants to remove the hairs and so begins to shake the vase when a second man with healthy eyes passes by. Surprised by his behaviour the second man approaches and looks at the place where the strands of hair are supposed to be. He sees no hairs and therefore does not form any conception of their existence nor non-existence, of a hair or a non-hair, or even of any of their attributes such as the darkness of the strands of hair. When the man suffering from the visual distortion tells the second man about his idea of seeing hairs the second man may want to correct his mistake by telling him that the strands of hair do not exist.

The Tibetan term translated here as "visual distortion" is *rab rib*,[20] which in turn translates the Sanskrit term *timira* originally used by Candrakīrti. It refers to a specific eye disease nowadays known as *myodesopsia*, sometimes also referred to as *vitreous floaters*.

The cause of this disease is that individual pockets of the vitreous humor, the gel-like substance that fills the eyeball, liquefy, eventually causing the production of small fibers in the gel. The shadows these fibers project onto the retina are then perceived as small, grayish, out-of-focus threads or dots in the visual field. These floaters are not stationary. Despite their name they

Candrakīrti

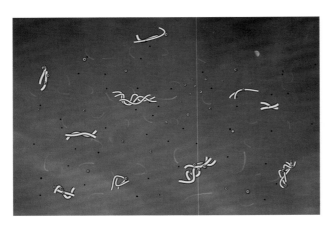

Appearance of
vitreous floaters

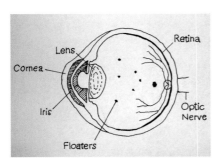

Floaters in the eye

do not float but have a tendency to sink toward the bottom of the eyeball. This perception of small threadlike objects is the reason why the Indian tradition says that a symptom of the *timira* distortion is "the appearance of falling hairs." In fact it is only because these floaters move that we perceive them at all. Other parts of the eyeball, such as blood vessels, obstruct light as well, but since they are always at the same place, information about them is filtered out by the brain and is no longer perceived.

Vitreous floaters belong to a class of visual illusions called *entoptic phenomena*. Unlike the familiar optical illusions and many forms of hallucinations, which are brought about by the way in which our brains process visual information, entoptic illusions have their causes within the human eye, so that at least these causes, if not the actual phenomena, can be observed by another person. (An ophthalmologist looking into your eye will be able to see the pockets of liquefied gel in your eyeball, but they will not look to her the way floaters look to you.) This is the same distinction as that between objective and subjective cases of tinnitus. In the first case a sound (such as that made by the pulsation of the blood) can be heard as coming from the patient's ear, whereas for subjective tinnitus the sound can only be heard by the sufferer himself.

Apart from floaters other examples of entoptic illusions are vascular images, which are the perception of the retinal blood vessels when light is shone into the eye from an unusual angle (which often happens during ophthalmic examinations); the "blue field illusion," which is the appearance of small bright dots caused by white blood cells in the capillaries in front of the retina; as well as pressure phosphenes, the flashing multicolored lights one sees when pressing one's eyeball. Interestingly enough some anthropologists have suggested that some of the patterns seen in upper palaeolithic art may be explained as depictions of such entoptic phenomena.

Two facts are particularly interesting about vitreous floaters. The first is that they are very widespread. Most people have experienced floaters at some time. You will probably have some too. The best way to observe them is to lie on your back and look at the sky. This will concentrate the floaters at the back of your eyeball, close to the center of your gaze. Looking at an empty monochrome background such as the sky also makes floaters particularly easy to see.

Second, even though there are various physical treatments available, such as removing some of the gel which fills the eyeball, or trying to destroy the floaters with lasers, these are usually not very effective. Floaters are either not completely eliminated or come back again. For this reason the most promising treatment appears to be one that does not actually try

An invisible gorilla

to take out the impurities within the eyeball but focuses instead on the *perception* of the floaters. Taking into account that virtually everybody has floaters but that only some people find them irritating, annoying, or even debilitating, it makes sense to assume that those suffering from floaters have an increased sensitivity to a condition most people have but that does not greatly affect them. In order to help those suffering from floaters it is therefore useful to attempt to change their perception of floaters.

The idea here is not that the patient continues to see the floaters but is no longer bothered by them, but, more interestingly, that the patient no longer perceives the floaters at all. This is done by exploiting the brains marvelous ability of selective attention and inattention. Objects that are not at the focus of our interest might literally be invisible to us.

This was demonstrated in a very impressive fashion by an experiment in which psychologists showed subjects a short video of students playing with a ball. There were two teams, wearing black and white T-shirts, and the subject's task was to count how many times the ball was passed between the members of the white team. In the middle of the video an actor dressed up in a gorilla suit walked through the picture, stopped in the middle, and pounded his chest. If questioned afterward whether they saw anything odd, as many as half of the candidates turned out not to have seen the gorilla. This sounds hardly credible, but it indicates how much of our visual perception is based on where our attention is directed, rather than just on what happens in front of our eyes.

But if our brains are able to filter out the gorilla right in front of us, it should also be possible to use this very ability to filter out objects we do not want to see, such as floaters. In this way, even though floaters are a distortion within the eye with a clearly observable cause, it would be possible to cure it by purely psychological means, not by eliminating the cause (which is not what the patients find irritating in the first place) but the perception of the cause, which is the real basis of the suffering experienced.

It is interesting to note that vitreous floaters are a very popular example in Buddhist philosophical literature, so popular in fact that they are used by many different authors to make different points. I think the two properties of floaters we have just discussed, the fact that they are very widespread and that they can be dissolved in a purely cognitive way, are the explanation for this popularity. Let us look at this in a bit more detail.

Candrakīrti continues his discussion of floaters as follows:

> The man not suffering from visual distortions sees what the strands of hair are really like, while the other man does not. In the same way there are those suffering from the visual distortion of ignorance, so that they are incapable of perceiving how things really are. The substance seen by them is nothing more than a conventional form. The blessed Buddhas, on the other hand, are without any trace of such ignorance, so that they perceive the hairs like one who does not suffer from the visual distortion.

What the ignorant ones do not perceive, according to Candrakīrti, is the *emptiness* of all things. Emptiness is one of the most important and also most intricate terms within Buddhist philosophy. In order to understand what it means we have to ask ourselves what things are supposed to be empty *of*. The emptiness the Buddhists are interested in is the emptiness of substance. What is a substance? It is something that exists independently of any other thing, something that provides the foundation for other things in the world, though it does not itself have any foundation in any other thing.

A good example of a substance are the atoms described by the early Greek philosopher Democritus, who lived in the fifth and fourth centuries BCE. According to Democritus, the most fundamental things in the world were eternal atoms and the void in which they are arranged. Both are eternal, and the variety of things we see, hear, touch, smell, or taste are just different arrangements of atoms. When the things change, the atoms constituting them are simply rearranged, even though no atom passes out of existence. When we burn a piece of paper the paper ceases to exist, but the atoms

Substance depicted on a non-substance

cannot be destroyed and continue to exist in the scattered pieces of ashes. Nothing that is really real, that is, nothing that is a substance, can ever be destroyed.

Democritean atoms do not depend on anything. They do not depend on somebody or something making them, for they have no beginning. They do not depend on their parts, for they have none. They do not depend on our minds because they continue to exist whether we perceive them or not. I have chosen Democritean atoms rather than the fundamental particles physics presently studies as an example of substance, because it is still unclear whether these particles have the characteristics of substances. Even with a presently popular notion such as string theory it is not evident whether strings really are the "rock bottom" of the physical world, and, even if they are, whether the existence of one string is independent of that of any other one.

If Democritean atoms are an example of substances, what is an example of something that is not a substance? Many things: the cup on my desk, for example. It is composed of many particles of matter, and if these particles did not exist anymore the cup would not exist either. So the cup depends on other things for its existence and is not a substance. And even clearer example is money. Money is obviously not the coins and notes in your pockets— these are just representations of money. Money itself is something that only exists because of the agreement among a group of people to treat something as money. If they stop regarding it as such (as, for example, we no longer regard cowrie shells as carrying monetary value), it will stop to be representing money. So money cannot be a substance because its existence depends in a very clear way on human minds and the conventions they collectively observe.

Now when Candrakīrti and his fellow Buddhists say that everything is empty, they are trying to say that there are no substances. There are no Democritean atoms, nor are there any other things that could fulfill their function. Whether that implies that, like money, all things only exist by social agreement is quite another question.

The most important point in our present discussion of illusions is that the Buddhist philosophers do not regard the discussion of whether or not substances exist as a purely theoretical one that is of importance only so long as we do not leave our armchair. For them the purpose of determining the existence or nonexistence of substances is not just to arrive at a theoretically satisfactory understanding of the fundamental objects that make up everything there is, but is supposed to have far more comprehensive implications for how we interact with the world. The realization of the nonexistence of substances is supposed to bring about a cognitive shift, a different way of seeing the world, which will ultimately also bring about the cessation of suffering, one of the fundamental characteristics of existence.

According to the theory of emptiness, substance is not regarded as a theoretical posit, as something a philosopher might postulate when investigating the world or its representation in language. The underlying idea here is rather that seeing objects in terms of substance is a kind of cognitive default that is criticized by the Buddhist's arguments. It is important to realize that the notion of substance is seen here as playing a fundamental *cognitive* role insofar as objects are usually conceptualized in terms of substance.

According to this cognitive understanding, substance is regarded as an illusory superimposition that the mind naturally projects onto objects when attempting to conceptualize the world. Independent of one's particular theoretical position concerning the existence or nonexistence of substance, substance is something that is superimposed on ordinary objects in the process of conceptualization. The different elements that make up a person, a body, beliefs, thoughts, desires, and so forth, for example, are seen as a single, permanent, independent self, due to the superimposition of substance on such a basis. The same happens when ordinary material things that have parts are apprehended as single, permanent, independent objects.

It is because this cognitive default of the superimposition of substance is seen as the primary cause of suffering that the Buddhist philosophers draw a distinction between the *understanding* of arguments establishing emptiness and its *realization*. Being convinced by some Buddhist argument that substances do not exist does not usually entail that the things will not still appear to us as being substances or at least as being based on substances. The elimination of this appearance is only achieved by the realization of emptiness. The ultimate aim of the Buddhist project is therefore not just the establishment of a particular philosophical theory, but the achievement of a *cognitive change*. The elimination of substance as a theoretical posit by means of arguments has to be followed by its elimination as an automatic cognitive superimposition by means of specific practices.

This distinction between understanding and realization can be made more clear by considering an example from mathematics. When doing geometry we usually study the three dimensions of space: its width, depth, and height. But there are parts of mathematics that study spaces with more dimensions than three—the so-called higher-dimensional geometries.

Suppose we study a world with four spatial dimensions and want to investigate what properties cubes have in such a world. It is possible to prove various facts about a four-dimensional cube without having any idea of what such a cube would look like. We simply regard it as a theoretical entity that is defined in a certain way, and then proceed to prove further facts on the basis of this definition.

On the other hand could also try to develop a spatial intuition for the fourth dimension, that is we could try to get an idea of what such a cube would look like. This could be done by a simple exercise. Imagine a set of beings living in a space with only two dimensions, on a flat plane with no height. Now consider how a three-dimensional cube looked to them. How could these flat beings get an idea of a three-dimensional object? Once we understand how *they* can know a cube in a space with one dimension more than the one they live in, perhaps we can use an analogous procedure to visualize a cube with four dimensions. A three-dimensional cube passing facedown through a two-dimensional plane would appear to these flat beings like a square. They could now try to visualize the cube as a sequence of such squares. Similarly a four-dimensional cube passing

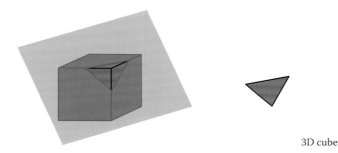

3D cube

through our world would look like a three-dimensional cube. If we change the orientation of the object passing through, the shapes get more interesting. A cube passing through a plane with a point first would appear like a triangle that first increases in size, the shrinks again until it disappears:

If we try the same trick with a four-dimensional cube we get a sequence of objects like this:

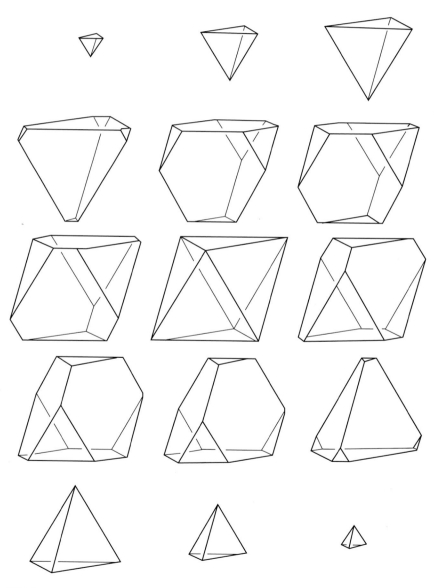

4D cube

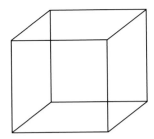

Projection of 3D cube

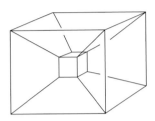

Projection of a 4D cube

We could therefore try to imagine a four-dimensional cube by considering different sequences of three-dimensional objects, corresponding to a four-dimensional cube passing through our space in different ways.

Alternatively we could consider a projection of a four-dimensional cube into three dimensions. When we draw a normal cube according to the rules of perspective we end up with the projection of a three-dimensional object into the two-dimensional space of the painting. An analogous "perspectival drawing" of a four-dimensional cube in two dimensions would look like the lower drawing on the left. As a normal cube consists of eight squares put together, the four-dimensional cube consists of eight three-dimensional cubes. In the model we can see that there is a big cube with a smaller cube inside. Furthermore there are six cubes around the inner cube that connect it to the bigger one. Due to the laws of projection they are distorted so they look like six pyramids with their tips removed. All cubes are of the same size but are distorted due to the projection. Unlike our near-automatic ability to read projections from three dimensions (that is, perspectival drawings), interpreting projections from four dimensions takes some getting used to. There is, however, no fundamental difference between the two.

A final, somewhat quaint (and labor-intensive) way of developing our spatial intuition for the fourth dimension was devised by the British mathematician Charles Howard Hinton (1853–1907). Hinton (who was also the inventor of the first—and only—gunpowder-powered baseball pitching machine) marketed a complex set of eighty-one multicolored wooden cubes, representing the eighty-one parts of a four-dimensional cube three units long. These cubes had to be used to assemble various three-dimensional structures, taking into account various congruities between surfaces, edges, and colors. One would then memorize these structures and begin to move their different parts against each other in one's mind. In the end these cognitive exercises would allow the diligent student to perceive the fourth dimension directly.

It is clear that trying to enlarge our spatial intuition in the ways described is not just about proving theorems about higher dimensions, but requires

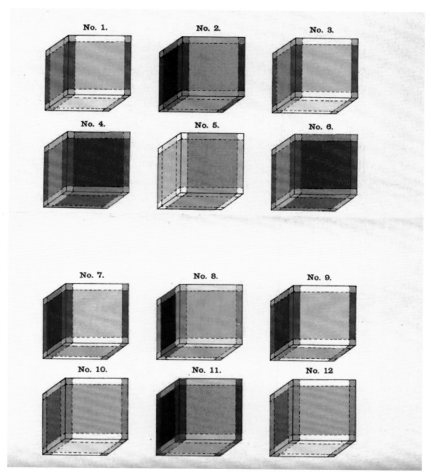

Some of Hinton's cubes

certain exercises for enlarging our imagination. In the same way the Buddhist's attempt to remove the superimposition of substances in things is not just about working through philosophical arguments, but also requires certain exercises to effect a cognitive shift that keeps the mistaken projection of substances from occurring.

But is there any evidence that we unconsciously superimpose the notion of a substance onto our experiences? Buddhist philosophy generally assumes that this superimposition applies to two things: to the self and to other phenomena we encounter. I talk about the superimposition of the self elsewhere in this book, so let us now concentrate on the other objects around us.

There is certainly evidence of a default in human cognition that achieves two things. Firstly, all other things being equal we conceive of a sequence of stimuli as corresponding to a single enduring, though changing, object, rather than to a sequence of different, momentary ones. Secondly we usually assume an external rather than an internal object as the source of the stimulus. Let me call these the *principle of permanence* and the *principle of externality*.

The principle of permanence ensures that we generally conceive of objects as enduring phenomena that may change over time, but still remain fundamentally the same object, rather than as unrelated, momentarily arising and ceasing phenomena, each of which lasts only for an instant. There is nothing logically deficient about interpreting the information we receive through the senses by seeing things as momentarily arising and ceasing, but it is just not the way we see the world. There are good reasons why we do not do so, primarily that such a representation is vastly too complex to use in practice. Any mind that lived in such a world of kaleidoscopically flashing phenomena would be at an evolutionary disadvantage when compared to one that represented a world of stable, enduring objects.

The principle of externality makes us assume that the causes of sensory experiences are objects lying outside of us, rather than the product of our own perceptive mechanisms. We generally assume that our perception is evidence for things located outside of ourselves and that we do not live in a hallucinatory world of our own devising. Again, such a principle makes evolutionary sense: running away from an imaginary tiger is not as detrimental to our chances of passing on our genes as is declaring a real tiger rushing toward us to be a figment of our imagination.

If something appears to us as a substance it has to appear both as permanent and as observer-independent—if a substance could be produced and destroyed just like ordinary objects, there would have to be some cause or other that was responsible for this. But then its existence would depend on this cause, so that it could not be independent. But what is dependent cannot be a substance. In particular something that depends for its existence just on us (like a hallucination) or on a group of minds (like a contract) cannot be a substance, since it would only be there if the mind or minds in question existed too.

Let us look now at two simple results from cognitive psychology that could serve as evidence that something like the two principles of permanence and externality play an important role in our cognitive access to the world.

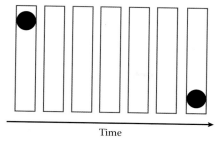

Time

What is shown

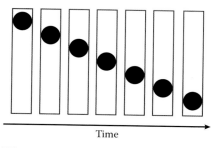

Time

What appears

The first, the so-called beta phenomenon, has been known to experimental psychologists for a long time. The subject of the experiment is shown two slides, the first of which contains a dot in the top left-hand corner, the other a dot in the bottom right-hand corner. What the subject perceives if these slides are shown in quick succession is not two stationary dots, but a *single* dot moving diagonally from the top left to the bottom right across the slides. What has happened here is that the subject's brain has interpreted the sequence of two stationary dots as a single moving object that is first seen on the left and then on the right. Rather than interpreting this particular stimulus as one object appearing at one spot and immediately disappearing, followed by another object appearing at a different spot, the principle of permanence causes us to see the two dots as a single object changing its position in space. When offered the choice of either regarding some sequence of stimuli as corresponding to a series of momentarily arising and ceasing objects, or as an enduring object changing its attributes, our brains seem to opt automatically for the latter.

Further interesting results were obtained by the psychological study of reactions to stage magic. Here subjects were shown a simple magic trick: a stamp was put into the box, the box was then closed, and when it was opened again a different stamp was in the box. This kind of situation seems to violate the principle of permanence, since it looks as if one object had vanished without a trace while a different one suddenly appeared in its place. When asked to explain what they had seen subjects generally offered theories that did not conflict with object permanence. They suggested that some chemical reaction happened in the box, that the experimenter had hypnotized them and exchanged the stamp himself, or even that he was able to influence the stamp by sheer willpower. In each case the stamp or stamps involved could be thought of as enduring objects that change over time.

The principle of permanence seems to be a central assumption presupposed by most of our thinking about the world.

Some evidence for the principle of externality can be drawn from the psychological investigation of dreaming, in particular of the phenomenon of lucid dreaming. A lucid dream is a dream in which the dreamer is conscious of dreaming but does not wake up. Although lucid dreams happen spontaneously to some people there are also a variety of techniques for inducing them. But the fact that some special effort is required to have a lucid dream points to the fact that our natural reaction to perceptions in dreams is to regard them as caused by external objects, rather than by our own minds. So it seems that our view of sensory information both in the waking state and in the dream state is generally determined by the principle of externality: in both cases we regard the source of the information to be something that is both external to us and existing independently of us. It requires a particular cognitive effort to question in a dream whether the things one sees are indeed caused by external sources, an effort that appears to be essential in inducing lucid dreaming.

If it is plausible to understand the Buddhist notion of superimposition of substance in terms of certain cognitive defaults (such as the principles of permanence and externality) that govern our representation of the world, then it becomes clear why the Buddhist philosophers draw a sharp line between intellectual understanding and realization. The superimposition of substance onto a world that in fact lacks it can be compared to the illusion of vitreous floaters because this illusion is on the one hand very widespread (*all* beings see the world in this distorted way) and can on the other hand be overcome by a cognitive shift. The most severe case of illusion in this context would be the man described by Candrakīrti, who thinks that the floaters he sees are external objects, such as strands of hairs. Once this illusion is cleared up, that is, when the man is convinced by arguments that the floaters he sees are a product of his eye, not of the world, he nevertheless continues to see the floaters. According to the Buddhist understanding most beings suffer from the most severe kind of illusion—they think there really are substances out there. Those convinced by the arguments that there are no such substances are a bit less deluded: they have acquired an intellectual understanding but no realization yet, because the world still *seems* to them as it appears to everybody else, even though they do not take this appearance at face value. The realized being, finally, is the equivalent of one who does not even see floaters any more: his mind has stopped the superimposition of substance onto things. But if there is no appearance of either things or persons existing, as the Tibetan authors often put it, "from their own side," there can be no more grasping at these things, because both the grasper and the grasped have disappeared. Since this grasping is what the Buddha regarded as the principal cause of suffering, once grasping has disappeared, the cessation of suffering is obtained.

A MIRAGE

སྒྱིག་རྒྱུ

THE *Discourse on the King of Meditations*, a fourth-century Buddhist text, remarks the following on the topic of mirages:

Know all phenomena to be like this:
At noon in midsummer,
a man tormented by thirst, marching on,
sees a mirage as a pool of water.
Know all phenomena to be like this:
Although a mirage contains no water,
confused beings will want to drink it.
But unreal water cannot be drunk.

According to the Tibetan tradition a particular class of spirits, called *yi dag*,[21] or hungry ghosts, suffers this illusion frequently. To be reborn as a *yi dag*, it is claimed, one must have a mind filled with greed. These hungry ghosts confront a nightmarish world where their desires are continuously thwarted. Their physiognomy matches their situation; they are depicted with huge bloated bellies but minuscule mouths and throats. Their necks are barely able to support their heads and their arms and legs are as thin as stalks. Their bones are wrapped in their skin like a log in a bag of dry leather.

Tormented by constant hunger and thirst, they travel far and wide to find food and drink and are exhausted from their travels. In the rare instances when they find a piece of food it vanishes in front of their eyes, or if they succeed in grasping it, it transforms into excrement into their hands, or if they swallow it, into fire in their mouths. When they see a distant lake to quench their thirst as soon as they get there it turns out to have been a mirage, and

Hungry ghosts seeing illusory water

all they find is the dry sands of a desert.

Mirages do, of course, not just appear to hungry ghosts but to human beings as well. They provide us with a particularly interesting example of an illusory phenomenon. Few people know that there are two fundamentally different kinds of mirages that, for reasons that will shortly become more clear, are called *inferior* and *superior* mirages. The illusory pool of water seen in the desert belongs to the inferior type. Let us see how this comes about.

Light waves travel at different speeds in different media. The speed of a beam of light passing through air is different from one passing through water, which is again different from one passing through a piece of glass. When light passes from one medium into another one where it has to travel at different speed, its direction is changed. The beam of light will be bent, a phenomenon known as refraction. (For a more detailed explanation of how refraction comes about see pages 126–28). This is why a pencil half-immersed into a glass of water will look crooked: the light reflected by the part of the pen under water will reach our eyes at a slightly different angle than that reflected by the dry part.

What causes a mirage is first of all the fact that the density of air varies with its temperature. Cold air is denser than hot air, so light travels more slowly in cold air. Secondly we need layers of air with different temperatures close to one another to produce a mirage. One case in which this comes about (which is in fact the situation giving rise to inferior mirages) is when the ground is heated up by the sun, so that the air close to the ground is warmer than the air higher up. Note that what is important here is the *temperature difference* between the different layers of air, not the temperature of one layer in itself. As such the layering of air necessary for a mirage can as easily occur "at noon in midsummer" in the middle of a desert as it can on a

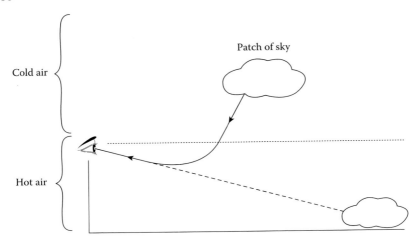

How an inferior mirage happens

cloudless winter day. For a mirage to occur we need a temperature difference of seven to nine to five degrees Fahrenheit per yard. As a matter of fact, even greater temperature differences are quite common once the sun heats up the ground.

The above diagram illustrates how an inferior mirage, like seeing a lake in the middle of the desert, can come about. Light from a particular patch of sky will travel downward. When it moves from the colder and more dense layer of air higher up into the warmer layer closer to the ground it starts to bend. This bent light ray finally reaches our eyes. As light rays usually travel in straight lines we do not expect this one to have come from high up in the sky, but from the point where our line of sight (indicated in the diagram by the broken line) meets the ground. This is because in normal circumstances, when light rays are not bent, it would be light reflected from this spot that would reach our eyes when we are looking down, so that we would see whatever is located at this spot. Due to the unusually bent light ray from the sky, however, we see a bright blue spot somewhere down on the ground. It is now clear why this phenomenon is called an inferior mirage, because we see the object, in this case the patch of sky, below its real position.

As layers of air of different temperatures are usually not stable, the bending of the ray of light will change to some extent while we observe the mirage. The blue spot in the distance will therefore seem to vibrate a bit. Since an extended, somewhat moving blue spot on the ground seen in the distance is in fact a lake more often than not it is easy to understand why in this situation we think there is some water where there really is none.

An inferior mirage

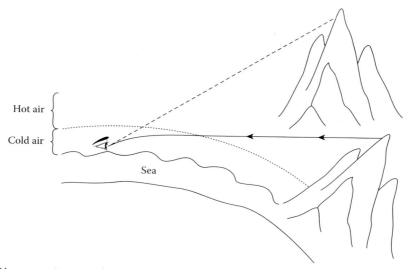

Hot air

Cold air

Sea

How a superior mirage happens

The second kind of mirage, a superior mirage, occurs when the layers of air with different temperatures are arranged the other way around: the cold air is close to the ground, while the warmer air is higher up. This situation is more likely to occur in arctic climates, or at sea. In this case the light ray is bent the other way around, as can be seen from the following diagram.

Imagine you are standing on top of a ship in the middle of the ocean. At a distant coast there is a high mountain. The air close to the surface of the sea

A superior mirage

is relatively cold, while it is warmer higher up. If the temperature difference is great enough, the light rays reflected by the top of the mountain will bend downward when entering the colder, lower layer of air until they reach your eyes. But once again you will not expect these light rays to have come from where they have come from, but from somewhere intersecting with your line of sight. It therefore appears to you as if the top of the mountain was floating somewhere in the sky, above the horizon. As the image appears above the real location of its cause, this is called a *superior mirage.*

Superior mirages are particularly interesting because they sometimes let us see things we normally could not see, because they are located behind the horizon. A straight light ray obviously cannot go around the curve of the globe, but a bent one can. We can observe this phenomenon every morning at sunrise. In this case the reason for the bent light ray, however, is not a difference in temperature but the fact that the light of the sun is bent when leaving outer space and entering the comparatively dense atmosphere of the earth. Because the light of the sun is bent downward we perceive the solar disk to be about half a degree higher up than it really is. (This is also roughly the diameter of the observed solar disk.) We therefore see the sun about two minutes before it actually climbs above the horizon.

Taking into account the meteorological conditions of India it is clear that inferior images could be observed far more frequently than superior ones. This explains why the mirages referred to in Indian texts, as well as in the Tibetan texts based on them, are always of the inferior variety.

In order to understand what makes a mirage illusory it is useful to think of it under three headings: the *existence* of water, the *appearance* of water,

Asaṅga　　　　　　　　Vasubandhu

and the absence of water. When confronting a mirage without realizing it is a mirage we mistakenly think that we face a real body of water existing somewhere in front of us. The peculiar atmospheric conditions bringing about the mirage produce in us the belief in the existence of water where there is none. Unlike the water, however, the atmospheric conditions themselves are of course perfectly real: there really is a vibrating blue patch projected onto a part of our retinas. The appearance is real, even if the appearing object is not. Finally, despite its appearance the water is really absent from where we see it. There is no lake where we perceive it, as we will find out if we try to reach it and want to drink from it.

Mirages are often used as a philosophical example in writings from a strand of Buddhist philosophy known as *Yogācāra* (frequently called "mind-only school" in English texts). The central works of this school were composed in third- or fourth-century India by two brothers called Asaṅga and Vasubandhu.

They argued that *all* phenomena had to be understood in the same way as a mirage. The three headings of existence, appearance and absence had to be applied to all things in order to comprehend their nature.[22] At first this might strike us as a rather bizarre idea. After all there seems to be all the difference in the world between a real lake, in which we can bathe and swim, and a mirage, which has none of the properties of a real lake (apart from one, namely that it *looks* like a real lake). So how can we make sense of the claim that ordinary phenomena have the same nature as a mirage?

---

22. This is the famous *Yogācāra* theory of the "three natures" (*trisvabhāva*).

A real lake

Consider a real lake, such as the one in this picture, located in eastern Bhutan at an altitude of more than 16,400 feet.

We assume that this lake *exists* as a physical object somewhere outside of us, can be seen by other people (not only ourselves), and does not depend for its existence on us looking at it or thinking about it. But if we reflect for a moment we realize that all our knowledge of the lake depends on our mental representation. We cannot get the lake into our heads, and not even the light rays it reflects can get into our minds. All we are dealing with when we speak about the lake is a representation, an *appearance* of a particular blue spot in our visual field that has a particular size, a particular brightness, and so forth. All of this is doubtlessly there, but we do not think of the existence of the lake as mind-dependent in this way. We do not speak of representations in our minds, or images on our retinas (roughly speaking, of things "in here"), but of an object existing several miles away from our heads and far larger than it. It seems to us as if we directly perceive an object "out there," even though what is really happening is that our minds are carrying out a fairly complex construction from a variety of visual data, building a cognitive object to which a particular size, shape, color, and orientation is ascribed, a cognitive object that is then projected outward. Even though it seems to us as if the lake was "coming into" our minds, in fact the lake is what "goes out," based on an input of very disparate appearances that bear very little resemblance to a lake.

Now a key claim of the mind-only school is that, as in the case of an inferior mirage, the lake is really *absent*. Even if we cannot do otherwise than to conceive of what appears to us as being an external object "coming in," that is, as causing our perception, in fact there is no such object. There is no real lake, only various mental states dressed up in such a way as to give the impression of an external object. In the end, there is only mind.

In order to understand the claim of the miragelike illusory nature of things a bit better it is helpful to draw a parallel with an approach within the theory of knowledge called *phenomenalism*. Phenomenalism was a relatively popular theory in the twentieth century; in its earliest form it goes back to the works of the nineteenth-century British philosopher John Stuart Mill. The problem phenomenalism tried to address is this: We are faced with two conflicting beliefs. As we saw above, on the one hand we never have any direct contact with the external causes of our experiences but can only access them via their mental representations and cannot even form an intelligible conception of what such external causes would be. On the other hand we still think of the world as containing objects, such as tables and chairs, existing independently of all mental representations. So how can we avoid the unwelcome conclusion that almost all our beliefs about the world we live in are false? Despite the fact that I can never make direct contact with the cup, and there might not even be a cup out there, I would still like to argue that my belief that the cup is to the left of the teapot is true, whereas your belief that it is to its right is false. The falsity of your belief could be easily demonstrated if you attempted to pour your tea into the nonexistent cup.

The phenomenalist's interesting idea is that we can salvage the truth of most of our beliefs by giving up the world. We have to understand that our belief about the lake or teapot in front of us is not at all about physical objects, but about sensory experiences. When I speak about the present teapot I really mean my current experience of the sight of its color and shape, the smell of the tea, the sound of its lid being lifted; when I speak about the teapot yesterday I really mean the sensory experiences I had then. And when I consider buying a teapot I have never laid my eyes on I think about the experiences of the teapot I *would* have if I were to buy it. The phenomenalist replaces external physical objects with more or less stable possibilities of sensory experiences. It is now easy to see that my belief that the cup is to the left of the teapot is true not because there is either a cup or a teapot out there related in a particular way, but because an attempt at pouring the tea to the left will result in a tea-in-the-cup experience, while any attempt to pour to the right will lead to a tea-on-the-tablecloth experience.

We can now apply this idea to the mind-only view of all things being similar to mirages. What the phenomenalist suggests is conceiving of all phenomena under the heading of *appearance* only. We completely disregard that we usually experience them as *existent*, that is as mind-independent physical objects "out there." Viewing phenomena as existent will lead us to all sorts of false beliefs, since we could not possibly have any access to such mind-independent objects. At the same time we cannot act by just focusing on the absence of external objects. We do after all have to interact with the appearances in order to live in the world.

So assuming we accept the mind-only school's view that all things have to be conceived under the same three headings as a mirage, could we actually distinguish a real lake from an inferior mirage? The answer is that we can, or at least that we can in most contexts. If we were a painter wanting to paint a lake in the desert a mirage would do as well as a real lake, since all we would be after is the visual experience of the lake—and this is the same in both cases. But we normally interact with things in more than one way, for example we might want to drink from the lake, or to swim in it. In this case the mirage will provide us with different possibilities of experiences (if we jump in, we feel only sand) than the lake (if we jump in, we will feel the cool water). So even in the absence of the real lake "out there" it would be possible to tell the illusory mirage-lake from a nonillusory lake.

An obvious question anyone inclined toward a phenomenalist view of the world is likely to face is this: "Why are there all these more or less stable possibilities of sensory experiences? Why is it the case that when I looked down into the valley yesterday I had a lake-experience, and that when I look today I have one too? And why is it that if *you* look down into the valley you are going to have an experience that, as far as I can tell, is very much like mine? Is not the easiest explanation of this intricate pattern of sensory experiences that *there is a lake out there* that different perceivers perceive at different times?"

The mind-only school attempts to address this question by introducing the notion of a "foundation consciousness." This foundational mind (called "consciousness which is the basis of all"[23] in Tibetan), which is nothing else but the *appearance* of phenomena, is the only thing that truly exists. Everything else, the tables, chairs, lakes, and teapots of the world around us, is just a manifestation brought forth from it, like waves from an ocean. The mind-only school argues that the foundation consciousness is influenced by our actions. The actions deposit seeds within it that later, when bringing out their potential, result in new appearances. The amazingly complex web of sensual experiences is therefore not just a brute fact, something we cannot possibly explain. It is in a quite literal way the collective creation of beings experiencing these appearances, resulting from the potentialities they have deposited in the foundation consciousness by their earlier actions.

---

23. ཀུན་གཞི་རྣམ་ཤེས་

According to the Buddhist mind-only school the foundation consciousness, which is precisely the collection of *appearances* of phenomena, has the potential for bringing about both the world of suffering as well as liberation from suffering. Superimposing external objects onto the appearance, that is, conceptualizing the world under the heading of *existence*, leads to an attempt to cling to these objects and results in frustration because of their insubstantiality, just like suffering awaits the traveler in the desert who thinks there is a real lake behind an inferior mirage. On the other hand conceiving of phenomena under the heading of the *absence* of an external mind-independent existence will keep us from trying to grasp at them, so that finally the end of suffering will be accomplished.

Now all this implies that suffering can be stopped by changing the way things seem to us and, since there are no underlying external objects that are the causes of appearances, changing the way things *seem* to us is changing the way things *are*.

That the pleasure or displeasure we see in a situation is heavily dependent on the way in which a situation appears to us is a phenomenon that has been studied to a considerable extent in economics. The part of microeconomics called *rational choice theory* investigates how people should make decisions in order to accomplish the result most desirable to them. Put simply, it considers a set of possible outcomes of a given decision, each rated in terms of how much pleasure (or how little displeasure) we would derive from it if it came about. It also takes into account the different courses of action open to us, the pleasure or displeasure connected with these, and the probabilities that a particular course of action will lead to a particular result. For example, if we want to choose between different fire insurance policies we will consider how high the premium for each is, how much it would pay in case of a claim, and also how likely it is that our house will actually burn down.

Let us now consider the following interesting example. It concerns a group of patients suffering from lung cancer who had to decide between two kinds of treatment: surgery or radiation. In order to do so they would have to consider how painful each course of treatment would be to them, how highly they valued the results (that is, being able to live for some more years), and, of course, how probable each kind of treatment made such a result.

The table on the next page shows the probabilities involved. One group of patients was told that 90 percent of patients live through the operation, 68 percent of those undergoing surgery would be alive after one year, and 34 percent would be alive after five years. With radiation 77 percent are alive after one year, and 22 percent after five years.

The other group was informed that with surgery 10 percent die during the operation, 32 percent die within one year, and 66 percent die within five years. Choosing radiation 23 percent die in the first year, while 78 percent die in the following five years.

The curious fact now is that out of the first group 82 percent chose surgery, while in the other one it was favored by 53 percent. As we can exclude the possibility that one group was significantly more afraid of surgery than the other one this result is puzzling, because the statistical information given to the two groups is *exactly the same*. It is only presented in different ways: the statistics are explained to the first group in terms of chance of survival, to the second group in terms of chance of death. Even though one's fate is the very same if one has a 90 percent chance of survival or a 10 percent chance of death, for some reason the patients considered the situation described in the first way much more preferable, so that a significantly greater number favored surgery.

Now according to classical decision theory the cancer patients presented a clear example of irrational behavior. Decision theory subscribes to a *principle of invariance* that says that how much you prefer a certain outcome should not be influenced by the way in which this outcome is described to you. According to this principle the cancer patients are as irrational as someone who prefers a stack of twenty five-dollar bills to two fifty-dollar bills, as if the former were somehow worth more than the latter.

It has nowadays become apparent, however, that such "framing" effects are common in real-life decision situations. It is therefore not very satisfactory to consider them just as examples of irrational behavior. After all, a good theory

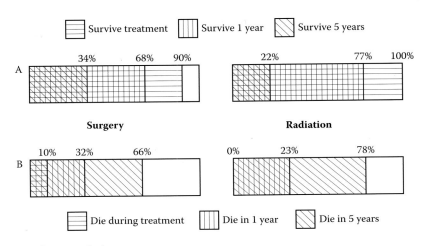

Survival statistics for lung cancer

of how rational beings should choose should not regard a significant amount of the choices they do in fact makes as irrational. Framing effects are something to be explained by a theory of rational choice, rather than an oddity to be ignored.

One natural way of accounting for framing effects is by rejecting one of the basic assumptions of choice theory: that the various outcomes are objectively existing situations independent of human cognition. One possibility of explaining what happened in the case of the cancer patients is that the different groups constructed different outcomes depending on the different ways in which the statistics were presented to them. For the patients in the second group, surgery was explicitly connected with death, which made it much less appealing than radiation. In the first group the outcomes were not conceptualized in terms of death at all, instead, both options had a high probability of surviving the treatment: 90 percent in the case of surgery, 100 percent in the case of radiation. In addition, the long-term survival chances were considerably higher in the case of surgery, so that for the first group this seemed to be the more preferable option.

According to this view the world does not come already sliced up into different situations or outcomes that we then desire to achieve or avoid. Rather these outcomes are something human beings construct. As such the statistical data in our example are mere *appearance*, what really concerns us in our deliberations is the *existent* situation superimposed on it. This has the interesting consequence that we can influence the pleasure or displeasure experienced by changing the way in which we frame situations. How we regard a particular scenario is not dependent on any of its intrinsic features, but a product of the way it is conceptualized on the basis of appearance.

We now see how regarding phenomena as comparable to mirages alerts us to two fundamental facts about them. First, the idea we have of phenomena as external, mind-independent objects is a conception superimposed on a complex array of sensory items all of which are both internal and mind-dependent. All we have on the level of *appearance* are more or less stable possibilities of sensation. That there is anything "out there" producing the sensation is an idea we can only arrive at by a leap of faith or, as the Buddhist would want to claim, by a deluded mind. For if the mind-only school is right there are no *existents* behind the *appearance*, as there is no water behind the mirage.

Second, the suffering or pleasure we experience is determined to a crucial extent by the way in which we superimpose *existents* on *appearances*. As we saw in the example of the lung-cancer patients the situations we experience as agreeable or disagreeable are not just out there, but depend to a crucial amount on the way we construct these situations ourselves. And when there is nothing behind the appearances, we can change the world by changing the way the world appears to us. Of course this does not mean that suffering can be avoided just by suitable reframing of appearances. A person who thinks that a mirage-lake contains freshwater might be more happy now than one who thinks that it contains saltwater, as the first enjoys the prospect of quenching his thirst. Ultimately of course both will be disappointed, as neither will find anything to drink. To avoid suffering, the Buddhist points out, it is not just sufficient to superimpose a different kind of lake onto the mirage, we have to realize that there is no lake whatsoever behind it.

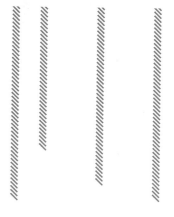

A DREAM

རྨི་ལམ་

IN 1687 Sangye Gyatso,[24] the regent of the fifth Dalai Lama, commissioned a series of seventy-nine paintings to illustrate an encyclopedia of Tibetan medical knowledge he had just composed, a treatise called *The Blue Beryl, ornament of the intention of the Medicine Buddha, which explains the Four Tantras.*[25] This text is a commentary on the Four Medical Tantras,[26] the principal textbook that all Tibetan medical students have to master before becoming physicians.

Three sets of these paintings are known to be in existence today, one in the Tibetan Medical and Astrological Institute in Dharmsala, one in the Dalai Lama's former Summer Palace in Lhasa, and one in the Buryat Historical Museum in Ulan-Ude. Some of these are anatomical paintings, showing the human body subdivided into squares by a grid of lines, some show the development of the human embryo or illnesses caused by imbalance of the humors. Most, however, are made up of long rows of tiny pictures stacked on top of one another, illustrating plants, stones, and metals to be used in medicine, pictures of medical instruments, and pictures of a variety of diseases. Two particularly interesting paintings depict signs seen in dreams. According to the Tibetan view of the human body dreams arise from the movement of consciousness through the body together with the life-sustaining breath (སྲོག་རླུང་). As some dreams are said to be the result of the blockage of different channels in which this breath is supposed to travel, which are in turn caused by humoral imbalances, the study of such dreams is of considerable diagnostic importance. For it is just such imbalances the physician will set out to rectify in order to cure

---

24. སྡེ་སྲིད་སངས་རྒྱས་རྒྱ་མཚོ་, 1653–1705.

25. གསོ་བ་རིག་པའི་བསྟན་བཅོས་སྨན་བླའི་དགོངས་རྒྱན་རྒྱུད་བཞིའི་གསལ་བྱེད་བཻ་ཌཱུར་སྔོན་པོའི་མ་ལྲི་ཀ།

26. རྒྱུད་བཞི།

The Regent Sangye Gyatso

the disease. The diagnostic meaning of these kinds of dreams will not always be what we expect. A dream of a lotus growing from one's heart, for example, is an inauspicious dream, indicating a disease of blood and bile, while dreaming of a burning fire, of a lake, or of being besmeared with blood foretell longevity and health free from disease.

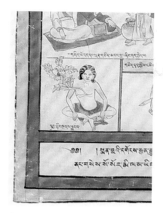

An inauspicious dream

An auspicious dream

The use of dreams as a diagnostic tool will not be unfamiliar to readers, even though in the Western world it is predominantly employed for the diagnosis of diseases of the mind, and even in this case only by the proponents of specific psychological theories. But apart from this diagnostic use there is another way the Tibetans use dreams that is not so familiar, and that is of particular relevance for the investigation of dreams as an example of illusion.

In the Tibetan tradition we find a set of meditational exercises commonly known as the Six Yogas of Nāropa.[27]

Nāropa was an eleventh-century Indian Buddhist saint. He was known as a great scholar at the Buddhist university at Nālandā in northern India but also as a *mahasiddha*, a tantric practitioner. These practitioners are usually described as rather eccentric and non-conventional characters who have obtained a number of special abilities (like being able to fly, or being clairvoyant) by their practices.

One day as Nāropa was reading the scriptures a *dākinī*, a sky-walking female spirit, appeared to him in the form of an ugly old woman. She asked him whether he only understood the words of the text he was reading, or their meaning as well. Nāropa, being a good scholar, said he understood the words—the woman laughed with joy. But he understood their meaning as well, he added—there the woman wept. She wept, she said, because she was sad he told such a lie. Then she disappeared, "like a rainbow in the sky."

Being very upset by this encounter, Nāropa later heard in a vision about the great teacher Tilopa. Nāropa became convinced that only through Tilopa's teachings he would attain complete enlightenment, so he undertook great hardships in first finding Tilopa, and later in being accepted as his disciple. He stayed with him for twelve years, and attained enlightenment in this very life.

Nāropa attracted many disciples from all over India. However, his most influential disciple was a Tibetan called Marpa (later the teacher of the famous Milarepa), who brought Nāropa's teachings of the Six Yogas back to

27. ན་རོ་ཆོས་དྲུག

The Mahasiddha Nāropa

Tibet where there they have been practiced ever since, thus surviving the eventual decline and disappearance of Buddhism in India.

Probably the most well-known meditational exercise from the Six Yogas is the practice of *tummo*[28] or inner heat. This is a complex set of visualizations and breathing exercises aimed at influencing different parts of the body as conceived by the system of traditional Indian physiology, which was later adopted in Tibet. According to this view "winds" or subtle energies, which are vehicles of consciousness, travel through the body via a network of channels. The aim of the practice is to cause the subtle energies to enter the central channel, which is supposed to lead to various profound states of consciousness conducive to the attainment of enlightenment. These exercises are so well-known because of an interesting side effect, namely that of allowing the practitioner to raise his body temperature by a considerable amount in a short span of time, a phenomenon that has recently also been the subject of some empirical studies.

A perhaps less spectacular but equally interesting set of practices concerns dreams (*mi-lam*, རྨི་ལམ་). These comprise a set of exercises that are supposed to enable the practitioner to influence the contents of his own dreams. After a set of preliminary procedures including vizualizations and breathing exercises performed while awake, one is then able to choose the contents of one's own dreams. For example one can decide to visit the celestial paradises of the Buddhas Maitreya and Amitābha, Ganden (དགའ་ལྡན་) and Dewachen (བདེ་བ་ཅན་), where lotuses grow that shine with radiant beams of light, where there is a perpetual

28. གཏུམ་མོ་

29. Interestingly, Tsong kha pa remarks in his commentary on the Six Yogas that "the pure realms experienced are mere reflections of the real thing. It is not that easy to experience the actual pure dimensions." It is tempting to speculate about what the difference between an actual and an imaginary travel to these celestial paradises might amount to.

rain of flowers, where the trees are decorated with gold, and where rivers of perfume flow.[29]

Rain of flowers in Amitābha's paradise

Besides being able to choose what to dream about the dreamer should also be able to transform the content of whatever he sees in his dreams. For example, if he dreams of fire, he can transform it into water, if he dreams of small objects he can make them big and the other way around, if he dreams of one thing he can multiply it to make many. If he wants to fly he can rise into the air. If he is afraid of fire in a dream he will know that dream-fire cannot burn, and will jump right into it. The fourteenth- and fifteenth-century Tibetan philosopher Tsong kha pa writes:

> When the practitioner sees a fire or flood in a dream and becomes frightened, he should think to himself, recognizing the dream: "How can the fire and water of the dream ever harm me?" Also, he should try to jump into the fire and cross the flood. To learn the illusory nature of dreams means to realize the non-existence of substantial existence of a vase and other objects of dream vision. This is accomplished by recognizing the dream. But one is not able, merely through the understanding, to realize the emptiness of substance of the dream. For instance, in the waking state, when one sees the reflection in a mirror, one knows that the reflection is illusory, yet one still cannot realize the nature of the reflection.

These ideas might well strike us as fantastic. After all our experience seems to show that dreaming does not work like that. We cannot choose what we would like to dream about, as we choose which film to watch at a cinema. We rather have to sit through whatever we are shown on the nocturnal screen, without the opportunity of leaving early if we don't like the film. Nor can we make the supposed magical changes to the dream's content. We are of course able to make certain choices in our dream, as we usually are the main actor in this internal performance. To this extent dreaming a dream is less like watching a film and more like playing a computer game. But we cannot do the magical actions suggested in Nāropa's dream yoga, any more than we can carry them out when awake. Or at least this is what we would think.

Recent research into sleep and dreaming has yielded some interesting results that are relevant in trying to understand the feasibility of Tibetan dream practices. Of particular interest in this context is research into lucid dreams. A lucid dream is a dream in which the dreamer is aware that he is dreaming. For people who have never experienced a lucid dream it is somewhat hard to imagine what this could entail. "Lucid" watching of a film (i.e., being aware that we are sitting in a cinema with lots of other people, looking a flickering lights projected onto the wall) tends to be rather unrewarding and boring. Similarly we might think that when we become aware that we are dreaming we might just "fall out" of the dream and wake up. But surprisingly this is not what happens. By "waking up in a dream" (as the experience of lucid dreaming is sometimes described) dreamers become aware of their ability to influence the contents of the dream.

One of the earliest extended descriptions of lucid dreaming is due of the Marquis Marie-Jean-Léon d'Hervey de Saint-Denys, a nineteenth-century autodidact sinologist who filled at least twenty-five notebooks with descriptions of his dreams, illustrated by himself. The notebooks are lost, but we still have the curious little book he published anonymously in 1867, called *Les rêves et les moyens de les diriger.*

This contains a brief history of the way dreams were seen in different cultures and also describes various events from his dream life. Here is a description of some of the feats he carried out in a dream.

> I dream that I am in a spacious room, richly decorated in an oriental style. Opposite the divan on which I am sitting is a large door enclosed by curtains of silk brocade. I think there must be some surprise hidden behind the curtains, and how pleasant it would be if they were raised to reveal some beautiful odalisques. Immediately the curtain parts, and the vision I desired is there in front of me. . . . I change a porcelain vase into a rock-crystal fountain, from which I desire a cooling drink—and

Hervey de Saint-Denys

this immediately flows out through a golden tap. Some years ago I lost a particular ring whose loss I felt deeply. The memory of it comes to mind, and I should like to find it. I utter this wish, fixing my attention on a piece of coal that I pick up from the fireplace—and immediately the ring is on my finger. The dream continues in the same way until one of the apparitions I have called up charms and captivates me so much that I forget my magician's role and plunge into a new, more realistic, series of illusions.

We might think that it is in principle impossible to investigate such phenomena as lucid dreams by scientific means. After all the lucid dreamer is the only witness of such events, and for all we know he might make it all up. So how can we arrive at anything like objective information about lucid dreaming?

A fascinating experiment was conducted at the University of Hull in the 1970s during which for the first time something left the dream world and entered the waking world. We are all familiar with the effect things from the waking world can have on the dream world: a cake we ate for dinner turns up again in the dream, the sound of our alarm clock is incorporated into the dream as the sound of a siren, and so on. But travel from the dream to the waking world is considerably more rare. That an object that we behold in a dream continues to be present the next morning in the waking state is something unfortunately confined to myths and legends.[30] The assumption that the connection between dreams and reality was a one-way street changed with the discovery that while most of our muscles are paralyzed during sleep (otherwise we would literally leap out of bed and act out the dream) the muscles that control the movement of the eyes are not. It was therefore possible to ask a subject in a sleep laboratory to move their eyes in a specific way (say five times to the right and five times to the left) in the dream whenever they became lucid. These movements could be recorded with special tracking equipment, and it could be confirmed that they indeed happened when the subject was dreaming.

---

30. One case of something moving from dream to reality, rather than the other way around, is that of nocturnal seminal emission as the result of sex in a dream. This case is frequently discussed in the Indian philosophical literature.

Frontispiece from *Les rêves*

This possibility of receiving signals from a dream in a systematic manner opened up the possibility of answering a whole range of questions that were thought to be beyond the reach of empirical research. A particularly interesting one concerns the notion of time in a dream. As any dreamer knows there can be a big difference between the time it takes to accomplish an action in a dream and the time the same action takes in real life. Intricate courses of events that seem to take years can take place in dreams lasting only half an hour. But now researchers could compare "dream time" and "real time" by asking a lucid dreamer to send a signal from his dream, estimate the duration of, say, ten seconds, and then signal again. (Interestingly it was found that the average duration of the period estimated during a dream was very close to that given when awake.)

The feats Nāropa's dream exercises advise us to perform are frequently carried out by people having lucid dreams. Furthermore, we are now in the position to investigate at least some aspects of lucid dreams by empirical (as opposed to purely introspective) methods. With the rise of empirical research into lucid dreaming there also appeared a variety of books teaching people how to achieve lucid dreams for themselves, either by employing some psychological techniques or by using electronic devices worn during sleep. It seems that the point of lucid dreaming thereby advertised is purely recreational: a cheaper and perhaps more enthralling substitute for watching a film or playing a computer game.

This, however, was not the motivation behind such techniques as those found in the Six Yogas of Nāropa. These techniques were meant as illustrations of a philosophical point, namely the equivalence of the dream state and the waking state. We read that "if one attains a mastery of this process, then, whether in the sleeping-state or in the waking-state, one realizes both states to be illusory." Employing these techniques can be regarded as a philosophical experiment, the aim of which is to provide a convincing example of claims about the nature of reality.

But what is actually meant by claiming that both states are equally illusory? It is easiest to answer this question by considering two particularly intriguing philosophical questions raised by dreams:

- What makes reality real and the dream illusory?
- Who is dreaming?

Let us consider the first question first. An obvious argument for the illusoriness of dreams is their utter bizarreness. In our dreams often one outlandish event follows the next, while during the waking state things proceed in an orderly, structured, and predictable manner. Our dreams might feature episodes like the Monty Python sketch describing the "Dull Life of a City Stockbroker," but our waking world is unlikely to contain a succession of spear-wielding Africans, naked newsagents, and murdered secretaries. What we experience when awake bears more resemblance to the real life of a city stockbroker, rather than to the pythonesque interpretation.

But this argument is not very strong. After all it could be the case that we led very exciting lives, including driverless taxicabs and homicidal monsters, but that our dreams contained nothing but predictable nine-to-five routines moving files from the in-box to the out-box. In this case the roles of illusion and reality would be inverted: our eventful waking life would be classified as a fanciful illusion, our nightly dream routine as solid reality. Nevertheless, we can probably find a better way of telling dreams from reality than just identifying what is real with what is dull. A recurrent characteristic of dreams is their lack of recurrence. Having woken up from a nightmare, drenched in sweat, just at the point when the masked assassin had cornered us in a dark cul-de-sac in foggy Whitechapel, we are relieved because we know we are unlikely to go there again. We might feel less relieved if we knew we had to watch the sequel of this nocturnal *film noir* the following night, but fortunately this is rarely the case. On the other hand, if we go to bed after a particularly animated party we can be guaranteed that the chaos in the living room will still be there next time we enter our waking state. We often escape the sequels to our dreams, but rarely manage to do so with the sequels to our lives.

The recurrence of waking life after repeated periods of loss of consciousness makes it very sensible to treat waking life differently from our dream life. There is little point in opening a savings account in your dream since you will probably not end up in the very same dream situation any time soon (if ever). But there are good chances that the bank account you open today in your waking life is still going to be there when you wake up the next morning.

But in fact this is not a particularly strong defense of the reality of the waking world either. To see why, consider the following thought experiment (or nightmare, according to taste). Assume you are a city stockbroker

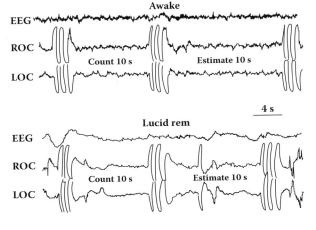

Comparing real and illusory time

in London in the 1990s. One night you fall asleep and after a short while have a dream that you are a student in Qing dynasty China, preparing for the Imperial Examination. You live through an entire day and after long hours of studying the Four Books and Five Classics you fall asleep. After a short while you wake up and find yourself in your London bed. A day of stockbroking follows, and you have barely fallen asleep when you dream about waking up on a *kang*, a raised Chinese bed, one day closer to the examination . . .

Now in this scenario of a long sequence of recurrent dreams it seems to be reasonable that even when you wake up in your London bed you still worry about your Chinese examination (supposing you can still recall it). For given the persistent nature of these dreams you will have to deal with the consequences should you fail the examination in some future dream. As you have no idea when your Chinese dreams are supposed to stop you'd better make sure you pass, for the very same reasons you make sure you do a good job as a stockbroker: in order to ensure a smooth running of events in the future.

The important point to get here (as with any philosophical thought experiment) is that we do not have to determine how likely such a sequence of recurrent dreams is, or whether it could happen at all. Rather we have to understand that in this counterfactual situation *as well as in the actual one* we draw the line between dream and reality on purely pragmatic grounds. It is not that our waking life is intrinsically more real or more weighty than our dreams, it is just that our waking episodes and our dream episodes are connected in different ways. Should these connections change, what we regard as real and what we regard as illusory will change as well. Dreams are not illusory by nature, nor is our waking life real by nature.

But if it is just our attitude toward certain groups of our experiences that decides which of them are illusory and which real (even though this may be influenced by the way in which some are more recurrent than others) then it becomes more understandable how Nāropa can regard dreams and reality as fundamentally equivalent. Both are sets of experiences arising from a complex set of causes that are partly internal and partly external. If anything, this is the nature that both share. The only difference between them is that we take one more seriously than the other. This fundamental equivalence is confirmed by the similarity of brain activity during the waking state and rapid eye movement (REM) sleep (when most remembered dreams occur). A recent empirical investigation of dreaming notes that

> we were able to account for the heightened sense of reality in dreams
> by hypothesizing that the brain is doing in the REM state essentially

the same thing it does in the waking state; a sensory input is being elaborated. In other words, the dream world is "real" because there is no detectable difference in brain activity.

Another way in which we can understand the equivalence of dream and reality is by looking at the dreamer, that is at the subject who dreams the dream. On the face of it, it seems to be obvious that it is the same "me" dreaming of the Whitechapel assassin and waking up safely in bed later. But if we reflect for a moment we realize that it is actually quite hard to say what we base this conviction on. We clearly cannot have any criterion of bodily continuity in mind here, that is we cannot appeal to the same criteria we would use when establishing that we are the same person tonight as we were this morning. In a dream we can have all sorts of bodies, which may be very different from the body we have in waking life, or indeed we may have no body at all. But equally we cannot refer to a continuity of memory as there are very few memories shared between the dreamer and the waker. Few remember much of their dreams when awake (though this gets easier with

London Stock Exchange

Examination cells

practice) and even fewer recall significant parts of their waking life in the dream (we might in fact argue that in order to do so it is necessary to have a lucid dream). It is this difficulty of establishing the relationship between the dream self and the waking self that caused the Taoist philosopher Chuang-Tzu to wonder whether he was a man dreaming of a butterfly, or a butterfly dreaming of being a man. In the same way we may ask whether the thought experiment given above could not equally be described as the recurrent dreams of a Qing dynasty student leading the life of a twentieth-century London stockbroker. It seems that asking which of these is the real self presents us with similar difficulties as asking whether the waking world or the dream world is the real world. Depending on your perspective a plausible case can be made for either one.

It is useful to remember at this point that according to the Buddhist worldview in which Nāropa is situated there is no such thing as a permanent self in the first place. The Buddha taught that human beings have the illusion of such a self, which is seen as the possessor of their bodies, thoughts, and memories, as the agent of their deeds, as the sufferer of their misfortunes, and as the beneficiary of their happiness. But apart from the individual parts that make up a person (her body, thoughts, desires, plans, intentions, and so forth), none of which is itself the person, there is no permanent entity that is the bearer of all of this. Now according to this view it is understandable why dream and waking life are regarded as equivalent when considering the nature of the waker and the dreamer. In waking life we mistakenly identify a waking self that we care about, that we want to protect from suffering and lead to happiness, and in the dream we mistakenly identify a different self (which is equally illusory) and burden ourselves with keeping *this* self happy and free from suffering. But of course none of these identifications is correct: there is no self in the dream and no self when we are awake either.

We therefore see that the study of lucid dreams in the Tibetan tradition is regarded as a way of illustrating two important philosophical points: that of the insubstantiality of the external world, and that of the insubstantiality of the self. The Buddha claimed that once these are really understood all suffering is ended. Because this understanding of insubstantiality can be brought about by the investigation of dreams, Nāropa called them the foremost of all the examples of illusion.

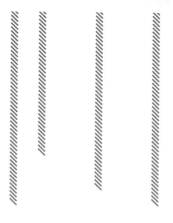

AN ECHO

 སྒྲ་བརྙན་

ON A HILL only a short distance away from the town of Hyderabad in southern India lies the ruined fortress-city of Golconda. Built in the twelfth century it stood for over five hundred years before it fell to ruins after being taken by the Mughal emperor Aurangzeb following a siege of nine months. Even what remains today is impressive; there are the remainders of the outer wall over six miles long, containing eight gateways and numerous bastions, enclosing the ruins of the royal palaces, bathhouses, women's quarters, storehouses, stables, wells, temples, and mosques inside. The unassailable Golconda fell through treachery. One of the outer gateways, now known as *Fateh Darwaza*, the "Victory Gate," was opened to Aurangzeb by a conspirator.

In front of this gate one can witness an impressive piece of early acoustical engineering. If one claps one's hands in front of the Victory Gate, the

Golconda Fort

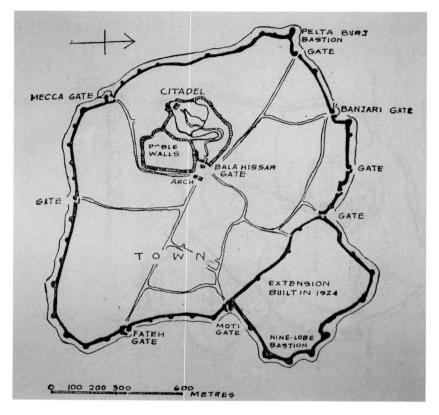

Plan of Golconda Fort

sound reverberates and after some seconds one hears one's clap again. More surprisingly, the clapping sound is still clearly audible at the Bala Hisar pavilion, the highest point of the fort more than half a mile away. The whole process also works in reverse. By a clever arrangement of walls between the gate and the lookout pavilion, sounds are redirected so as to travel from one to the other virtually undiminished. The underlying phenomenon behind this speedy communication device, which is extremely useful for a military fort, is the clever use of an echo, that is of the reflection and redirection of sound waves.

This is what the *Great Treatise on the Perfection of Wisdom* has to tell us about echoes:

When one is in a narrow valley, a deep gorge, or a vast house and one says something or makes a sound, the sound one has made will produce another sound, called "echo." A stupid man will think that there is somebody who repeats his words, but the wise man knows that the echo is no third person, but that it is solely by the reflection of sound that there is a new sound called echo. The echo is empty of reality, but it can still deceive the ear.

This passage gives a fairly accurate picture of how an echo comes about. The key is the reflection of the sound off some solid object. The sound, which travels as a wave of alternating pressure in air, propagates outward in concentric circles from its source. When it meets an obstacle the wave is reflected back and an observer at the location of the sound's source may hear it again after an interval. Knowing the speed of sound (about 371 yards feet per second) and the minimal duration that has to separate sounds so we can tell them apart (at least a tenth of a second) allows us to calculate the minimum distance of a reflecting surface to allow us to hear the sound. This is about 55 feet. Anything closer than that may also produce an echo but would not be perceived as such by us, since the sound and its reflection would be heard as merging into one.

As the following diagram illustrates, shouting at a cliff 371 yards away will produce an echo about two seconds later. In order to understand what is illusory about echoes we first have to give some thought to the nature of sound. Take as an example the sound made by striking a silver bell. We may think that the sound it makes is just one of the many properties of the bell, alongside its silver color, its weight, its shape, and so on. And as these properties are located where the bell is, so is the sound. We can then identify the bell's sound for example with its vibrating at a certain frequency, or with the disturbance this vibration creates in the surrounding air. All things considered conceiving of it in terms of disturbance in a medium seems preferable, because a bell might also be vibrating in a vacuum, but then it would cause no sound. Since both the vibrating as

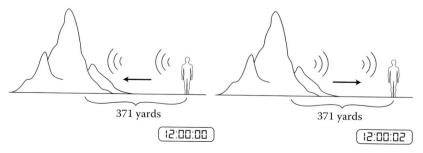

How an echo arises

well as the disturbance are located where the bell is this will be called the *stationary* view of sound. According to this view sounds do not travel. They will of course cause airwaves to travel and reach our ears, but these waves are not the sound, but merely a phenomenon caused by it. The sound itself stays at home.

A *mobile* view of sounds, on the other hand, holds that sounds do travel. The sound of the bell is something that starts at the place where the bell is and then travels outward from there, propagated by compression waves in the air surrounding the bell. Note that this does not necessarily commit us to identifying the sound with the waves, since we can also think that the sound is just what is transmitted by the waves without *being* the waves.

If we consider echoes it seems that these refute the stationary view of sounds. For when we hear an echo reflected from the wall of a cliff we hear it as located at that wall. This is why "a stupid man will think that there is somebody who repeats his words" because they appear to come from the other side of the valley. But the sound cannot be located at the cliff as the defender of a stationary view of sounds would like to think. The cliff does not vibrate, and thereby does not cause any disturbance in the air surrounding it. If we see sound as mobile, however, it is easy to explain what has happened: the sound carried by the airwaves moved toward the cliff, bounced off it, and has now returned to the location it came from. The sound is not located at the source but moves through space.

The problem with the mobile view, however, is that it does not accord very well with the way in which we *hear* sounds. We hear a sound as located close to its source. The ringing of the bell appears to be where the bell is. Moreover, we do not hear a sound traveling like a wave does, setting out from its source, getting closer, passing us, then continuing on its course. Neither standing in the sea and being pushed over by a water wave, nor feeling the wind (an airwave) come

Where is the sound of the bell?

from a certain direction is very much like hearing sounds, even though, if the mobile theorist is correct, they should all have the same underlying structure. We feel the wind coming toward us, but when hearing something we do not experience the approach of the sound coming from "over there" toward where we are. But if this is true then the only way in which we can locate things by their sounds, something we evidently do all the time with surprising accuracy, is by hearing the sound as located where the source is. Our experience of sound is that of stationary sound.

The view of sound as mobile seems to be unsatisfactory because it implies that we suffer from a systematic illusion both regarding the location of sounds, as well as regarding their duration. It appears to us as if the ringing of the bell is where the bell is, and on the basis of this we locate the bell by locating the ringing. But in reality sounds are moving through space, leaving their source, coming toward us, then passing by—but we are unable to perceive them the way they really are. Moreover, what we experience as the sound's duration does not correspond to its duration at all. We hear a sound as having a particular length by encountering the different spatial parts of the wave carrying it in succession: first the initial waves, then the middle ones, then the final one. But if the sound travels through space then it will have existed, carried by the respective airwaves, before it reached our ear, and it will continue to do so after it has passed them. So the *real* duration of the sound is the period during which the airwaves exist, not how long they take to pass us. This seems to be quite puzzling. For if we are systematically deceived about the duration of sounds, how do we manage to gauge the length of an event by the duration of the sound producing it? While the hand moves, the bell rings, and the duration of the hand's movement, we think, is just the duration of the ringing sound. This type of inference usually works very well. But if sounds were really mobile this would be a very surprising fact, as the duration of sounds and the duration of whatever is causing them have very little to do with one another.

If these difficulties convince us to embrace the stationary view of sounds and if we agree that sounds are located at their sources, how do we then account for echoes? As we have seen above, these are obviously not located at the place where they come from.

What the defender of stationary sounds should say is that when we hear an echo we do not hear a sound that has moved, but we hear the same sound twice. The sound is only generated once and stays where it is, but we experience it two times. Imagine there is an apple in front of you. Now put a mirror behind it, and a screen hiding the apple in front of it. First you will have seen the apple, then only its reflection in the mirror, as the apple itself is now hidden from view. The obvious thing to say here is that you have seen the same apple twice where it is, not that the apple has moved to the other side of the mirror after you put up the screen. Similarly we should say that the sound does not travel. When we hear an echo we experience one stationary sound twice because of the peculiar way its traces have traveled. But the sound remains where it is.

To use a slightly more fanciful example, imagine we put up a gigantic mirror in outer space, half a light-year away from Earth. As it will take one year for any visual information to get there and back we will be able to see in the mirror what happened one year ago on Earth. We are thereby able to see the same event twice, once in real time as it happens on Earth, and once a year later by the celestial replay. In this case it is obvious that the traces of the event (that is the light rays) will have traveled to the mirror and back, while the event itself stayed where it was.

Our reluctance to accept hearing an echo as hearing the same sound twice may be based on the fact that we are not very used to the repetition of events. The repetition of *objects* is commonplace: we see a cup today and a cup yesterday and identify it as one and the same cup seen twice. But the conditions for experiencing the same *event* twice are rare and typically involve complicated manipulations of mirrors of the type just indicated, or the ability to travel faster than sound. We therefore usually regard events with similar properties as distinct, while we tend to treat objects with similar properties as identical. But, the defender of the stability of motion will argue, such cognitive inclination has nothing to do with what sounds really are. That we are reluctant to identify the echo and the original sound as the very same thing, albeit separated by a time gap, and appearing at a different place does not imply that they are not identical after all.

If we now appeal to the example of echoes to decide between the two accounts of sound, the stationary and the mobile, we realize that our perception comes out as illusory in either case. As we already saw above if we think sounds move

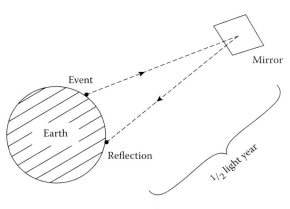

A visual echo

through space we have to accept that our perception of sounds as located at the source of the sound, and as lasting for the time we experience them, are illusory. The sound of the ringing bell is not where the bell is, but moves from the bell outward along the compression waves its vibrations cause. Nor does the sound of the bell last as long as the shaking of the hand that causes it to vibrate, but as long as the airwaves produced last.

If, on the other hand, we opt for the stationary view of sound it turns out that several of the perceived properties of echoes are illusory. We hear the echo as coming from the cliff, while it is actually located at the source of the initial sound. We hear it as happening as later than the initial sound, while in reality it is the very same sound as the initial one, only that its traces reach us at two separate times. And we might even think that sound and echo are two distinct objects, while they are really just one experienced two times over. According to this account we suffer from an illusion both regarding the space-time location of an echo, as well as regarding its identity.

When deliberating which view of sound should be regarded as correct we therefore cannot just opt for the one that provides us with a conception of sounds that matches our perceptions. We rather have to decide between two views, each of which implies that our regular auditory perception is based on illusions, either concerning sounds in general or concerning echoes in particular. Other things being equal we just have to find out which kinds of illusion we find less troubling, and then go for the account that implies these.

Now it is obvious that this choice is a purely pragmatic one. We select an account of sound that provides us with the greatest theoretical neatness and implies those illusions we are most happy to accept. But neither lets the way we experience sounds come out as corresponding to what the account says sounds really are. We should therefore consider neither account as an objective description of what sounds "really" are, but rather as a more or less satisfactory systematization of our experiences of them. And regardless of which systematization we choose, we cannot escape the fact that our experience of sounds involves a significant amount of illusion.

It is interesting to note that the *Great Treatise on the Perfection of Wisdom* continues its discussion by investigating another dimension of the illusory nature of echoes. This is the illusory appearance that an echo produced by some piece of speech involves both a speaker and a recipient. When you hear an echoed "hello" it seems as if somebody is greeting you.

The *Treatise* regards human speech as having an echolike illusory nature. From the Indian perspective this makes a lot of sense, as the common theory of how speech is formed assumes that it works very much like an echo. The idea was that when someone is about to speak he has a particular wind in his mouth that then travels down toward the navel. When it hits the belly an echo is produced and the sound is reflected upward, where it hits one of the places of speech production: the throat, the gums, the lip, the teeth, the tongue, the nose, or the chest. The sounds that leave the body afterward are experienced as speech. The *Treatise* continues:

> *Thus language is produced,*
> *the fool does not understand this,*
> *faltering, stubborn he brings forth aversion and illusion.*
> *But the wise one*
> *is not annoyed, does not cling,*
> *he does not make a mistake. . . .*
> *The sound which comes and goes manifests speech,*
> *but there is no agent—*
> *It is a magic trick:*
> *Who would think*
> *that this skeleton, this bundle of nerves*
> *could speak?*

The point made in this passage is this: suppose you face an echo-producing cliff and shout "You idiot!" After some seconds you seem to hear a sound from the cliff, someone shouting "You idiot!" Knowing that it is an echo you will not be annoyed by this, since there is nobody there at the cliff calling you an idiot. But, the analogy goes, human speech is similarly produced by an echo-effect. So why are you annoyed when another person calls you an idiot, if you are not annoyed by the echo?

There seems to be an obvious answer: in the first case there is an agent, and that is what we get angry at, in the second case there is none, and that is why we don't get angry. But perhaps matters are not quite so straightforward.

In 1966 the computer scientist Joseph Weizenbaum wrote a simple computer program called ELIZA. The program simulates a therapist; one can ask it for advice by typing in a question, and the program will then reply. The mechanism behind the program is disconcertingly simple. All it does in providing answers is try to break down the input into its grammatical components and then echoes them back substituted into ready-made phrases. Despite this simplicity the results are often interesting. Here is a conversation the author had with ELIZA.

Hello, I'm Eliza.

Hello.

How are you today. . . What would you like to discuss?

I would like to talk about illusions.

Come, come, elucidate your thoughts.

They are an interesting case, aren't they?

Are you sure?

Yes, I think they provide some interesting problems. . .

Do you really think so?

I do. Are you interested in illusions?

Why are you interested in whether or not I am interested in illusions?

I assumed you were interested in how the human mind works.

You're not really talking about me, are you?

Well, who are you anyway?

Would you prefer if I were not anyway?

What would that be like?

Are such questions on your mind often?

Eliza, I hope you don't mind my saying so, but I think you are an illusion too.

What makes you think I am an illusion too?

You sound like a computer.

We were discussing you, not me!

But what makes me different from a computer?

Have you asked anyone else?

Yes, but none of the answers convinced me.

Are you sure?

After a couple of exchanges ELIZA's responses tend to become a bit repetitive and sometimes don't make sense at all. Despite the fact that the program nowadays strikes us as somewhat primitive, back in the 1960s people exposed to it reacted quite strongly (worryingly so, we might think). There were numerous cases where subjects interacted with the program for some time before it became apparent to them that there was no real therapist replying to their questions at the other side of the computer terminal. More interestingly, in some cases the emotional involvement with ELIZA, the idea that the program showed interest or concern in the questions discussed, did not go away even after being told what ELIZA is and how it works. This assumption that the program functioned very much like we do, despite the explicit knowledge that it does not, subsequently became known as the ELIZA-effect.

The illusion underlying the ELIZA-effect, that is treating a simplistic piece of software as if it was a rational agent with beliefs and desires, appears to be connected with what is sometimes called "the intentional stance." This term, introduced by the philosopher and cognitive scientist Daniel Dennett, denotes one of the many ways in which we can see phenomena around us. Take a simple object like a thermometer. We can see it from a *material* stance, just as a physical object, a glass tube filled with mercury. Or we can regard it as something with a certain purpose, as a device made in order to measure temperature. This means seeing it from the *design* stance. When we see the thermometer from the *intentional* stance, we conceptualize it in terms of mental states, for example if we say that the thermometer knows that it is 74°F.

Some stances are more useful than others for understanding different phenomena: seeing the thermometer just as a glass tube ignores a lot of its complexity, while regarding it from the intentional stance presents us with plenty of pseudoproblems ("Where are the thermometer's beliefs stored?" "Can it draw inferences from them?" "Could a thermometer doubt its own temperature-judgments?"). So we would want to say that the illusory conception of both the person offended by the echo shouting "You idiot!" back at her as well as someone who feels understood by ELIZA's responses are based on seeing the echo-voice or the computer program from the intentional stance, a stance that is inadequate in these particular cases.

But how do we know which stance is the right one to adopt? We can imagine two different kinds of replies. A realist might say this: "Some objects, like sticks and stones, are just dumb pieces of matter. Others, like thermometers, clocks, tape, recorders or computers are artifacts: they were made by human beings with a particular purpose in mind—to measure temperature or time, to record sounds, to process information. A third group, like the people around you, and some animals at least, have desires and beliefs. If you meet an unfamiliar object, investigate it closely and you will find out which group it belongs to. Then you know what the correct stance is."

On the other hand someone else might say this: "That is not right, there is no such thing as *the* correct stance for each object. What stance you should adopt depends on what kind of ends you want to achieve. If you try to calculate how many people fit into an elevator it makes sense to regard them from the material stance. A biologist may see them from the design stance, as things that have a certain purpose, such as to survive and spread their genes. If you interact with them it is usually best to adopt the intentional stance. Sometimes it is useful to explain how a complex mechanism works by pretending it has beliefs and desires. Car mechanics do it all the time ('The engine *knows* it is getting too hot and therefore it *wants* more coolant"). And who knows, there might even be cases where it is useful to adopt the intentional stance toward sticks and stones."

If we consider ways of deciding a central question studied in artificial intelligence, namely how to decide whether a man-made artifact such as a computer is capable of intelligent thought, it becomes evident that the second view (that the stance adopted toward a given object depends on the end we want to achieve) seems to be the most popular one. The most well-known test is the so-called "Turing test," named after the mathematician Alan Turing, who designed one of the first computers. The setup is simple. The experimenter is connected by his computer terminal to two different rooms. In the one room is a human being, in the other is a computer. All communication proceeds by typing. The experimenter, who does not know which of the two participants is the computer and which the human, asks questions in order to find out. Both the human and the computer try to convince him that they are the human being. A computer is said to have passed the Turing test if, after a reasonable period, the experimenter is not able to say which is which.

The underlying idea is, obviously, that we regard a computer as capable

of intelligent thought, that is, as something that we see from the intentional stance if it manifests a certain behavior. The machine has to be able to respond in adequate ways and because it does so we decide that the best way to predict its future behavior is by seeing it from the intentional stance. What the computer is actually made of or how it is programmed is irrelevant. For all we know it might

Alan Turing

be a complex contraption made of Coke cans and pieces of string, but in this case the Turing test implies that we should adopt the intentional stance toward a pile of Coke cans. There is no need to "look inside" to see whether the thing is "really" conscious—after all we rarely look into our fellow beings to determine whether they are capable of intelligent thought. Normal interaction with them is usually sufficient to settle this.

That the stance with which we view phenomena should be chosen with reference to pragmatic concerns, rather than based on "what things are really like in themselves," is also suggested by the discussion of the illusory echo in the *Great Treatise on the Perfection of Wisdom*. The fool is annoyed by the echo insulting him because he sees it from the intentional stance. Seeing things in this way comes naturally to us, as the example of ELIZA shows. In that case even a minimal and restricted pattern of responses produced considerable emotional reactions. But if the intentional stance is not something demanded by the inner nature of the objects themselves, but is selected to facilitate our interactions with them, we can sometimes choose a different stance if this produces greater happiness. A man who sees the insults directed against him by another person as not different from those produced by a computer program or an echo may remain calm in the face of such invective and will not get angry. This is likely to be beneficial for both insulter and insulted, so that it appears to be a good thing *not* to adopt the intentional stance toward one's fellow being in this case. The wise man is therefore one who knows which stance is the right one to adopt in each case. Those suffering from illusion are the ones who adopt stances likely to lead to suffering, such as those thinking that the echo is speaking directly to them, as well as those who believe that in each case there is only one stance to adopt.

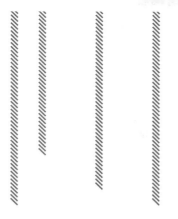

THE CITY OF GANDHARVAS

WHEN THE sun rises over the plains of India, and its rays illuminate the tips of clouds near the horizon, sometimes a strange sight can be seen. The *Great Treatise on the Perfection of Wisdom* tells us that in the sky

> one sees a city with rooms on the lofty tops of buildings and royal palaces, and moving people who go about in them. As the sun rises higher, the city fades away: it is nothing but a trick of light, devoid of reality. This is what one calls the city of Gandharvas. Those humans who have never seen it and who discover it one morning when looking eastwards believe it is real and quickly walk towards it. But the closer they get, the quicker it fades and, once the sun has reached a certain height it completely disappears. . . . The city of Gandharvas is not a real city, it is only human thinking which makes it so.

The Gandharvas who inhabit this marvelous city in the clouds (which is called *Vismāpana*, the Astounding One) are a refined race of mythical creatures. In Tibetan they are called *dri za* (དྲི་ཟ་), which literally translates as "scent-eaters," because scents are said to be their only nourishment.

The Gandharvas are renowned as heavenly musicians, which is why their king, Dhṛtarāṣṭra, whom the Buddhists regard as one of the guardians of the four directions of the world, is always depicted as playing a lute. They frequently leave their city to attend the god Indra in his heaven, entertaining the divine company with songs and music. The vast city of Vismāpana is pleasantly free from overcrowding. As the *Atharva Veda* informs us, there are only 6,333 Gandharvas altogether.

These demigods have particular power over women, such that in fact "their very presence provokes their hairs to stand up and thrills of unimaginable delight in females." Accordingly they are known to leave their celestial city to conduct all sorts of affairs with earthly women. In fact one Gandharva called Viśvāvasu is said to hold a *ius primae noctis* over every newly wed bride. In some Indian marriage rites a rod of *udumbara* wood (*Ficus glomerata*), wrapped in cloth and anointed with perfume representing this Gandharva, is placed on the bed between the couple for the first three nights after their marriage.

The Gandharvas' predilection for earthly women still manages to capture the Indian popular imagination. The last film of the Indian director P. Padmarajan, called *Njan Gandharvan*, tells the story of a female college student who finds a wooden statue on the beach that transforms into a Gandharva at night. Uncharacteristically, the Gandharva, who is always accompanied by the scent of *pāla* flowers, falls in love with the girl and decides he does not want to go back to his celestial abode. Needless to say, there is a tragic ending.

The city of Gandharvas is interesting as an example of illusion in more than one way. On the one hand its appearance as a city in the clouds is a rather picturesque example of mistaken perception. The edges of low clouds are illuminated by the rays of the rising sun and are mistaken for the skyline of a fantastic gold-colored city.

On the other hand this city is noteworthy as an entirely imaginary place that (together with its inhabitants) exists only in the human mind and its products, such as tales, poems, or pictures. The objects created by fiction are a particularly interesting case of illusory objects. Even though it is surprisingly difficult to say what, exactly, fictional objects *are*, it is

Dhṛtarāṣṭra, the king of Gandharvas

clear that they are often taken to be something that they are not, an essential characteristic of an illusory phenomenon. Each year about seven hundred letters are written to Sherlock Holmes at 221b Baker Street. In the past they were all delivered to the Abbey Road Building Society which occupied the premises stretching from 215 to 229 until 2002 and which used to employ somebody to answer each one as "Mr. Holmes's secretary."

Sherlock Holmes is obviously not a person who could answer a letter, nor is the city of Gandharvas a city one could visit. Nevertheless each exists in some way, and there are many true things we can say about them, such as that Sherlock Holmes claimed he traveled to Tibet or that the city of Gandharvas is inhabited by demigods. So what is the nature of these fictional objects?

ST. JAMES'S PALACE
LONDON SW1A 1BS

From: The Equerry to HRH The Prince of Wales

12th July 1994

Dear Mr Holmes,

Thank you for your letter dated 4th July, in which you kindly invite The Prince of Wales to visit the Sherlock Holmes Museum.

His Royal Highness will be holding a meeting at the end of November when his diary will be decided for the first eight months of 1995. I will ensure that your invitation is considered at that meeting and will be in touch in December with a decision.

I am only sorry that I will not be able to give you an answer before then.

Yours sincerely,

Major Patrick Tabor, RHG/D

Sherlock Holmes, Esq.,
221b, Baker Street,
London, NW1 6XE.

HRH The Prince of Wales writing to Sherlock Holmes

One might want to argue that it is misleading to assert that we can say anything true at all about fictional objects. This is so, it is claimed, because when we make an assertion about a real object we speak about the properties it has in our world, but in the case of fictional objects we only ever speak of them *in the fiction*. So when we say that it is true that there are 6,333 inhabitants of the city of Gandharvas, what we really mean is that the *Atharva Veda* asserts that there are just so many. So we do not actually say anything about an *object* at all, all we do is speak about *statements* that are made in a specific body of texts.

But this overlooks that we can make a number of true statements about fictional objects outside of fiction. For example we can say that Vismāpana, the Astounding One, has fewer inhabitants than Kāśi ("the Shining One," the old name for present-day Vārāṇasī), or that Sherlock Holmes is admired by many people in the twenty-first century. In these cases we are not speaking *within the fiction*, since Kāśi or people in the twenty-first century are not elements of the pieces of fiction we have in mind.

Moreover, if all talk about fictional objects just boiled down to talk about texts we face the difficulty of specifying which texts we mean. The *Atharva Veda* is not the only piece of literature mentioning the city of Gandharvas—in fact many of the mythical beliefs about it have never been written down. Sir Arthur Conan Doyle is not the only author who has written about Sherlock Holmes, but several other writers have done so since. What (this is unlikely, but not impossible) if we found out that another writer before Conan Doyle had also written about a detective called Sherlock Holmes? What if several of these texts contradicted each other?

We might therefore think that it is more satisfactory to treat fictional objects as theoretical entities. Atoms are one type of theoretical entities that physicists discuss. They are no more reducible to what all physicists have written about them than theoretical entities that literary critics discuss are reducible to what a bunch of authors wrote about them. This view seems to make more sense, but it commits us to ascribing rather strange properties to fictional objects. We all agree that there are some questions about fictional objects that do not have an answer. Did Sherlock Holmes have an aunt in Leamington Spa? None of the stories say that he did or he did not. Are there buildings in the city of Gandharvas taller than three hundred feet? Unfortunately none of the sources in Indian mythology go into that much detail.

Fictional objects are therefore distinguished from other entities, both from theoretical ones, like atoms, as well as from nontheoretical ones, like tables and chairs, by being *incomplete*. For every ordinary object, if we take any statement about it, it is either true or false (even if for practical reasons we could never find out whether it is true or false). But for fictional objects this is not the case. They have "holes"; there are aspects of them that remain indeterminate.

Some fictional objects are also contradictory. This happens when an author (usually inadvertently) makes inconsistent assertions about one of the objects he writes about. Dr. Watson is an example of a contradictory object. Conan Doyle claims that Watson has a war wound from being hit by a bullet during the second Afghan war in 1880. In *A Study in Scarlet* Conan Doyle claims this wound to be in the shoulder; in other places, such as *The Sign of the Four*, it is described as a wound in the leg. If we discount the theory that a single bullet went in at the shoulder and out at the leg, we are faced with a set of inconsistent claims. But while such inconsistency does not lead us to say that Dr. Watson does not exist, if someone describes an ordinary object as having two inconsistent properties we regard this as an excellent argument for denying that there is any such object.

An interesting perspective on the nature of fictional objects in general, and on fictional places like the city of Gandharvas in particular, is implicit in

Railway compartment with contradictory object

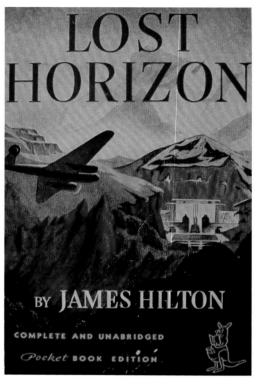

Plane approaching a hidden land

the Tibetan concept of "hidden lands."[31] These lands are paradisiacal realms, sometimes described as hidden away in some remote valleys of Tibet or the Himalayas. In these lands all flowers have the pleasant smell of jasmine and sandalwood, all plants have medicinal properties, the rivers flow with divine nectar, the air is perfumed by delicious scents, rainbows fill the sky, and need and suffering are unknown. Rather than being places for sensual enjoyment the hidden lands are regarded as ideal realms for Buddhist spiritual practice. In these realms even the birds speak of the Buddha's teachings, and passages from the scriptures appear miraculously on the leaves of plants and trees. Since the mundane cares of finding food, drink, clothing, and shelter in this world keep many from the practice leading to liberation, by entering a hidden land like this, so it is argued, the aim of enlightenment can be reached much more easily.

This idea of a Tibetan hidden land first reached a Western audience in James Hilton's novel *Lost Horizon*, published in 1933. It describes the crash of a plane somewhere in the Himalayan mountains carrying a British consul during the days of the Raj. The survivors find shelter in a monastery in an unknown valley where, mysteriously, men age more slowly than in the rest of the world. The monastery itself bears very little resemblance to Tibetan monasteries past or present. It comes equipped with central heating, green porcelain bathtubs, a grand piano, and a harpsichord, was founded by a Catholic priest from Luxembourg (the first to have translated Montaigne's essay "*De la vanité*" into Tibetan), and is presided over by an Englishman.

31. སྦས་ཡུལ་

Mandala of Shambhala

Critics have remarked that the description of the atmosphere at the lamasery of Shangri-La owes little to any Buddhist seat of learning and much to Oxford University.

Hilton's novel was based on what is probably the most famous of all hidden lands, the mythical kingdom of Shambhala, sometimes referred to in Tibetan as "the source of happiness."[32] Located at an inaccessible place in the Himalayas, Shambhala is said to have the shape of an eight-petaled lotus flower or an eight-spoked wheel. It is circular, surrounded by high mountains, and divided into eight districts. In the center is the capital city called Kapala where the king of Shambhala resides.

The mythical realm of Shambhala is intimately connected with a famous tantric text, the *Kālacakra Laghutantra*, since Dawa Zangpo,[33] the first king of Shambhala, is said to have requested this teaching from the historical Buddha as a way of practice that would not oblige him to give up his life and responsibilities as a king. Since then the text as well as the tradition of its practice, one of the most complex systems in the whole of Tibetan Buddhism, is claimed to be preserved in Shambhala.

It would be wrong, however, to infer that Shambhala was the only hidden land referred to in Tibetan literature. There is a long list of others, small or large, popular or obscure, supposedly located in various inaccessible regions of Tibet. Many of these realms are described in texts known as *terma*[34] or "concealed treasure." According to the Tibetan tradition the Buddhist teacher Padmasambhava hid a variety of treasures (texts, statues, images, and medical preparations) at different places in Tibet, predicting that they

32. བདེ་འབྱུང་
33. པ་བླ་བ་བཟང་པོ་
34. གཏེར་མ་

Lha'i Wangden, the Seventh King of Shambhala

would be found by specific persons at times of spiritual need.

One of the most peculiar genres of Tibetan literature is a set of texts called *lam yig*[35] or *ne yig*,[36] terms that mean literally "itinerary to the way" or "itinerary to the place." These itineraries are guidebooks to the hidden lands. At one level they read like ordinary guidebooks to pilgrimage places, describing the route, familiar landmarks, and the sights seen on the way, advising on the best way of planning one's journey, pointing out hazardous gorges, treacherous rivers, or dangerous passes. On the other hand they are also suffused with a mystical imagination, describing *ḍākinī*s, female embodiments of the Buddha's mind dancing in the sky, malicious demons guarding the hidden realm by producing illusions and miracles, winged lions, serpents with jaws the size of houses, walls made of crystal, and rocks engraved with auspicious symbols not made by human hands.

Here is a short excerpt from such a guidebook:

Beyond Menako he will come to the River Satvalotana, which flows from east to west with great turbulence and is extremely difficult to cross. It has fish of many colours with the faces of humans, tigers, lions, panthers, cows, monkeys, parrots, and other creatures. . . . Along the way the seeker will pass many springs, some of them poisonous, that issue from mountains filled with heaps of gold, silver, copper, iron, and other metals. . . . Passing beyond these springs, the seeker will come to five mountains covered with lovely flowers, trees, and jewels. Fabulous beings, both male and female, live happily there, playing with beauti-

---

35. ལམ་ཡིག་

36. གནས་ཡིག་

ful objects. They will sing enticing songs and make beautiful music to seduce the seeker. If that fails they will change into frightening forms and threaten him with terrifying sounds; or else they will produce various kinds of dismal smoke to make him sad and depressed.

This curious double nature of the itineraries to hidden lands, filled equally with factual information and mystical imagination, suggests that these lands should not be regarded as real places that we could visit in the same way as an ordinary, if slightly remote, village in a distant valley. The chances that we might accidentally walk into a *ḍākinī's* palace during a mountaineering expedition are slight. On the other hand treating hidden lands in the same vein as fictional places like the flying island of Laputa to which Gulliver traveled does not do them justice either. In English literature we do not even find one, let alone several, more or less plausible guidebooks that tell us how to get to this island of scholars.

In order to understand the Buddhist conception of hidden lands, and of fictional places like the city of Gandharvas more specifically, it is essential to note that in the Tibetan tradition the world is not regarded as a kind of prefabricated container in which human beings are placed and lead their lives. On the contrary it is something *brought about* collectively by a group of beings, in dependence on their specific karma.

This idea is illustrated well by a passage from a philosophical treatise called *The Twenty Verses*, composed in the fourth century by the Indian Buddhist writer Vasubandhu. In it Vasubandhu discusses the status of the guardians of the Buddhist hell realms. These guardians inflict terrible torments on the unfortunate beings reborn in hell, boiling them in molten metal, tearing out their tongues, impaling them on shrubs with thorns sharp as razor blades, and so on. According to the Buddhist view the hell-beings experience this suffering as a consequence of the nonvirtuous deeds

The Buddhist view of hell

done by them in previous lives. But the status of their tormentors is somewhat puzzling. They should in turn create terrible karma for themselves by inflicting all this suffering on the hell-beings. So there would have to be other hells where the guardians are reborn, and other guardians to torture them there, and then other hells where *these* guardians are reborn, and so forth. While not straightforwardly contradictory this view is certainly very uneconomical.

Vasubandhu evades this problem by denying that the guardians are real beings at all. These, together with the landscapes of hell, its burning mountains and icy deserts, lakes of fire and forests of thorns, are projections by a group of beings with a particular kind of mind. Because the hell-being perpetrated evil deeds, its mind is now shaped in such a way that it creates these hellish circumstances. Rather than thinking of beings being thrown into hell it makes more sense to regard them as creating their own hellish world, dependent of the deeds they have done in the past.

This view also allows us to make sense of the guidebooks to the Tibetan hidden lands. They are guidebooks insofar as a group following them will reach these lands, but they are no ordinary guidebooks because one will not see the hidden lands without the right kind of mind. As a certain kind of mind needs to be had to perceive the torments of hell, the treasures of the hidden land are similarly brought about by the minds of the people setting out to find them.

Coming back to the example of the illusory city of Gandharvas we realize that fictional places can be fruitfully regarded as collective projections. What creates the world of Sherlock Holmes is not the fact that the text of the stories has been written and now exists somewhere, but that people read these stories, talk about them, illustrate them, think about them, try to fill in the gaps in the stories, write biographies of Holmes and Watson, edit the *Baker Street Journal*, and so forth. If Conan Doyle's stories were only kept in a safe-deposit box and nobody ever read them, there would be no world of Sherlock Holmes. If references to Gandharvas disappeared from the Indian mythological imagination there would be no city of Gandharvas.

We may now conclude that what is illusory about the city of Gandharvas is that we regard a fictionally projected city as a real one. Or, and this seems more in keeping with the discussion just presented, we may conclude that the real illusion is to think that our world is so very different from the fictional city of Gandharvas. Our world, like a fictional place, may be a collective projection too, even if it is one of a more extensive and detailed kind.

If we reject the view of our world as a ready-made container that is the way it is, independent of what human beings think of it, and exists whether or not human beings exist, the apparently sharp distinction between a fictional world and the "real" one loses its solidity. Fictional worlds are created as a collective effort based on some kind of text or narrative. The creation of the real world is collectively brought about based on the sensory information entering our minds, and is highly underdetermined by it. It is influenced and shaped by the specific structure of our perceptual and cognitive systems, as well as by our interests, beliefs, and conventions. This underdetermination entails that the world thus created is not the only possible one. Any slight change in our perceptual and cognitive faculties, in our interests, beliefs, and social agreements might result in a radically different world, even if we assume an identical basis of perceptual data. The aim of the city of Gandharvas as an example of illusion is not so much to alert us to the error of mistaking a soft fictional world for a hard real one, but to point out the error of believing that the real world we live is any harder than a fictional one we see in the sky.

Even though the Gandharvas are usually regarded as demigods in Indian mythology they are sometimes seen very differently. In a monumental text called *Treasury of Knowledge*, Vasubandhu claims that the Gandharvas are in fact intermediate-state beings and that their illusory city is a dwelling in the intermediate state. According to the Buddhist view the mind enters this intermediate state after death, once it has been dissociated from the body, and remains in it until it has found a new body to be reborn in.

The Tibetan Buddhist tradition has developed a very detailed description of the intermediate state. It is set out in a text called *The Great Liberation upon Hearing in the Intermediate State*,[37] better known in the West as the *Tibetan Book of the Dead*.

The text describes how after the final moment of death there is the sudden appearance of a radiant clear light. Some time after that, during the next stage of the intermediate state, called the "intermediate state of suchness,"[38] the Gandharva experiences a confusing sight of lights and visions. It sees an elaborate array of forty-two peaceful deities that later transforms into one of fifty-eight wrathful deities, appearing as blood-drinking and flesh-eating demons.

---

37. བར་དོ་ཐོས་གྲོལ་ཆེན་མོ་
38. ཆོས་ཉིད་བར་དོ་

Mandala of Peaceful and Wrathful Deities of the Bardo

After these arrays have disappeared the final stage, the intermediate state of becoming,[39] begins. The intermediate being acquires an illusory body, comparable to the body that we think we have while dreaming. This body will have very acute sense faculties. Because this body is not material in nature the Gandharva is able to pass through rocks, walls, and other material objects without hindrance. It can instantaneously appear at any place it chooses and see and speak to the people it left behind. It may speak to its weeping relatives and say "I am here, do not cry!"—but they can neither hear nor see it.

The visions the Gandharva experiences at this stage become increasingly associated with the next rebirth it is going to acquire. If the previous deeds of the intermediate being cause rebirth as a human being, it will wander in the intermediate state until it comes across a copulating couple, which will then be its father and mother. If it develops desire toward the father and aversion toward the mother it will be reborn as a girl, if it is the other way around, as a boy. The intermediate being then unites with the fertilized egg in the mother's womb, acquires a body and thereby disappears.

The Tibetan tradition holds that if the intermediate being realizes during the intermediate state that it has died and is now in a state between its last and its next life, that the visions it sees are not real, that its body in the intermediate state is illusory, like a dreamer realizing in the dream that he is dreaming, it can attain liberation and escape the circle of life, death, and rebirth. For this reason the *Great Liberation upon Hearing in the Intermediate State* is read aloud next to the bodies of the recently died, hoping that the intermediate being, when it comes close to its former body, will realize what state it is in and obtain liberation.

It is interesting to consider what kind of being the Gandharva actually is. The Buddhist texts are very explicit in saying that there is no soul, no indestructible essence of a person moving from this life through the intermediate state to the next life. The *Śālistambhasūtra* even claims that "there is nothing whatsoever that transmigrates from this world to another world." A metaphorical illustration sometimes found in the literature attempting to show how a person, a Gandharva, and a rebirth can nevertheless be causally related is that of a die. The die makes an imprint; even if the die is then destroyed the pattern has been imprinted. But there is no piece of the die

---

39. སྲིད་པའི་བར་དོ

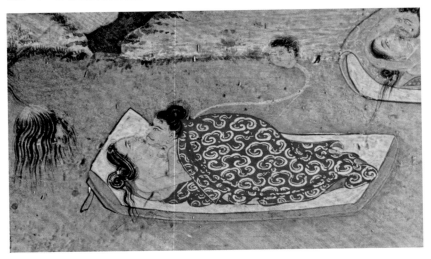

Gandharva finding a new rebirth

that is now also part of the imprinted pattern. In the same way a certain kind of mind, a karmic pattern, produces a person in this life, which then causes a Gandharva who has certain experiences in the intermediate state, which then in turn causes a person in the next rebirth.

I argued above that a good way of understanding why the city of Gandharvas is an interesting example of illusion is by seeing it as a fictional place. I would now like to suggest that it is plausible to understand the Gandharva, the self in the intermediate state, as a fictional object as well. It is a fictional character.

To see why this makes sense consider that what underlies our entire waking life is a constant internal monologue of thoughts. This monologue creates our self as the writings of Conan Doyle create Sherlock Holmes and Dr. Watson. If our consciousness continues after death, the monologue presumably continues as well, thereby creating the fictional character of the Gandharva, an intermediate being, of a similar character as the self we assume to have when dreaming.

A contemporary writer who defends this view of the self as a fictional character is the philosopher and cognitive scientist Daniel Dennett. According to his account the best way of understanding our internal monologue is not in terms of an author producing a piece of text, but of a text bringing about a fictional character, which happens to be the author. Dennett observes that "our tales are spun, but for the most part we don't spin them; they spin us. The human consciousness, and our narrative selfhood, is the product, not their source." For him there is no fundamental difference between selves and fictional characters, apart from the fact that selves are more open-ended: one's autobiographic monologue goes on, but most pieces of fiction have a clearly defined beginning and end.

But of course if we think that the Gandharva is an illusion because it is merely a fictional character, our reasoning will equally apply to the self that produced it, and to its next rebirth. I suggested earlier that the greater illusion might not be to see a fictional city in the clouds, but to think that the cities of this world are fundamentally different from fictional cities. In the same way a greater illusion than the Gandharva not realizing he is a being in the intermediate state might be that it does not occur to us that our selves are as illusory as the one the Gandharva thinks it has.

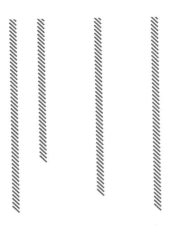

AN OPTICAL ILLUSION

མིག་འཕྲུལ་

OPTICAL ILLUSIONS can take a variety of forms. The one usually included among the twelve examples of illusion is the circle of fire.[40] This can be observed when a burning object, such as a torch or an incense stick, is whirled around in the dark. The various distinct positions it occupies in quick succession seem to merge into one, and we observe a single, glowing ring.

In the *Discourse of the Descent to Laṅkā*, which the Buddha taught in Laṅkā (sometimes equated with what is now Sri Lanka) after visiting the palace of the king of the *naga*s or sea-serpents, he says to the bodhisattva Mahāmati:

> Mahāmati, since the ignorant and the simple-minded, not know-
> ing that the world that is seen is nothing other than our own mind,
> cling to the diversity of external objects, cling to the notions of being
> and non-being, oneness and otherness, bothness and not-bothness,
> existence and non-existence, eternity and non-eternity, as being
> characterized by self-nature which rises from discrimination based
> on habit-energy, they are addicted to false ideas. . . . Mahāmati, [the
> world] is like a wheel of fire which is no real wheel but which is imag-
> ined to be such by the ignorant, but not by the wise.

The wheel of fire is no real wheel because it is a combination of two distinct illusions. The first is the *motion-blur effect*. This is easiest to explain by reference to a camera. The exposure time selected will determine how long the light reflected from the object will hit the unexposed film within the camera. If we photograph an object that moves during this time (such as a bouncing ball) the light bouncing off it will hit different parts of the film in succession. As a result we will not see a single dot on the film, but a sequence of dots merging into one another: a motion blur.

One way of avoiding the motion-blur effect is by using a stroboscope, that is by flashing a light very rapidly at the object. In this way the individual shapes projected by the moving ball are separated. We end up with the same image we would have obtained by taking forty-seven high-speed photos of the bouncing ball and then superimposing these photos onto a single photographic plate.

The circle of fire

The motion-blur effect also arises for our eyes. Of course these do not work like a camera by shooting a picture during a fixed exposure time. What happens is that the light hitting our retinas produces a set of impulses that is then passed on to the brain along the optic nerve. The continuous stream of information sent from the retina is interpreted by the brain in discrete

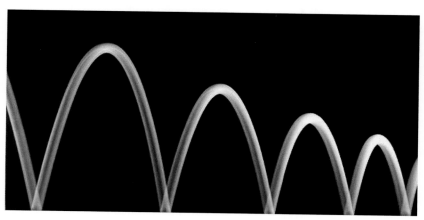

Blurred ball

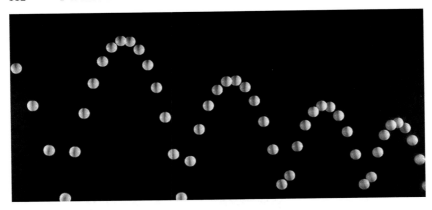

Stroboscopic image

packages, since sufficient information has to be collected first to allow for interpretation. The time required to put together such a package is called "integration time." Each of these packages can be regarded as an image. If an object moves very fast between the different integrations forming such images it will appear blurred, just like objects moving during the exposure time of a camera.

The temporal resolution of the human eye is relatively high. A bright flickering light can be perceived as flickering if it flashes up to a hundred times per second. This means that we are able to distinguish visual events as short as ten milliseconds (that's one-thousandth of a second) in extreme cases. On the whole, however, we are most likely to perceive a flicker if the light goes on and off between ten and thirty times per second. For a TV set to be perceived as "flicker free" it has to refresh seventy-two times per second. But this also implies that the motion-blur effect cannot be the only cause of the wheel of fire. Admittedly the integration time varies with light intensities. If there is less light, and thereby less visual information available, it takes longer to put together a visual image. In this way even relatively slow motions can produce a considerable blur in dim lighting conditions.

Nevertheless, even if we assume a very low temporal resolution threshold of ten refreshments per second when observing the circle of fire in the dark, the man whirling the torch would have to achieve at least ten revolutions per second to let us see a closed circle of fire—faster than the rotor of a helicopter in flight.

In fact the motion-blur effect is enhanced by a *positive afterimage*, which is the second kind of illusion required for bringing about the wheel of fire. When you look steadily at a bright light, such as a naked lightbulb, for some time and then look away you will often see a bright form shaped like the lightbulb

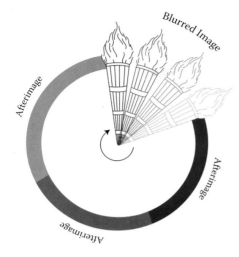

How the circle of fire comes about

projected onto whatever you are looking at. The explanation for this is that retinal cells continue to transmit a signal even though they receive no further stimulation. You therefore continue to see a bright light even though there is none present anymore. The opposite phenomenon, a negative afterimage, can occur as well, and usually succeeds the positive afterimage after a couple of seconds. In this case the retinal cell's receptivity to light is reduced in response to the bright stimulus, so that after the retina stops projecting the positive afterimage the area in question appears darker than it really is.

We can now see easily how the appearance of the wheel of fire is produced. While the torch is being whirled around it will move to a certain extent between different integrations of the information sent from the retina to the brain. We therefore do not see a single illuminated point (as we would if the torch was stationary) but a bright, somewhat blurry streak forming a part of a circle. This fragment of a wheel then creates a positive afterimage. What this means is that the retinal cells continue to transmit their impulses even after the torch has moved further along the circle. But just before the afterimage fades the light reflected from the torch hits this spot on the retina once more. A new stimulus produces a new impulse, which produces a new afterimage. In this way the entire circle is made up of presently observed blurred streaks and afterimages of such streaks seen in the past. We therefore have the illusion of a stationary circular object at a place where there is only a point in motion.

In essence this is also the explanation that Isaac Newton proposes in his *Opticks*. He notes that

> when a coal of fire moved nimbly in the circumference of a circle makes the whole circumference appear like a circle of fire, is it not because the motions excited in the bottom of the eye by the rays of light are of a lasting nature, and continue till the coal of fire in going round returns to its former place?

The ancient Indian illusion of the circle of fire seems to have found a new incarnation in a rather peculiar gadget known as a spinning LED clock. Here a row of light-emitting diodes (LEDs) is fixed on a rod that is then rotated like a propeller. By rapidly changing the pattern of LEDs that light up, the image perceived is not just a glowing circle, but an entire clock face with two hands seemingly projected into thin air.

Both illusions creating the circle of fire, the motion-blur effect as well as the positive afterimage, give rise to interesting questions on their own.

The motion-blur effect can be explained by some object moving so much during the integration of the image from our retinas that it only leaves a blurred image. But now imagine something moving much slower, such as a man going past the window. Such an object can be seen in a perfectly clear way. At one moment the light reflected by him hits our retinas at a specific set of points. This information is integrated into an image. After this has taken place the light will hit the retina at a slightly different spot, since the man has moved a bit during the interval. This having been integrated as well, it will hit still another spot and so on. But if this was the case we should perceive motion either as blurred (if the object moves fast) or as gappy (if the object moves more slowly). In the example above the walking man should first be seen at one spot, then there should be a tiny gap where he is seen to disappear (between the integration of two successive images), then he turns up again at an adjacent spot, and so on. Of course we perceive nothing like this—the motion of the man walking down the street appears perfectly smooth to us.

In fact the same problem arises when we watch a film on the cinema screen. A standard movie projector will show twenty-four different frames per second. Because each frame has to be "pulled down" to make room for the next as the reel goes through the projector, the shutter closes briefly while the frames are changed. In fact the shutter may go down two or three times over the same frames, so you would see forty-eight or seventy-two frames per second, even though either half or two-thirds of these would show the same image. While the shutter is down, generally for about 0.0125 seconds between two images, the screen will be dark and there is nothing to see. Adding all these times together implies the rather intriguing fact that during a regular ninety-minute movie you and the rest of the audience will be sitting in pitch darkness for at least half an hour. Again, this is not what we experience. On the screen we see a smooth series of motion stretching for the full ninety minutes, rather than a shorter one diluted by numerous little periods of darkness. What is happening is that we see motion in a rapid succession

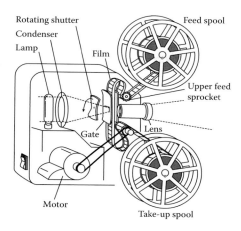

A film projector

of static views. This cinematographic illusion is the opposite of the circle of fire: there we were presented with a moving object, a torch being whirled around, but what we perceive is static: an immobile, flickering wheel of fire. In the cinema we are presented with nothing but static pictures, one still frame after another. Yet, inexplicably, what we perceive is a smoothly moving object projected onto the screen.

What is the explanation of the cinematographic illusion? A popular way of accounting for the fact that a cinematic projection shown at the right speed does not appear gappy is by reference to the *persistence of vision*. Here the idea is that the mind retains the image a little bit longer than it is actually perceived. Before it disappears a new image is already offered to us—this is why we do not notice the small intervals of darkness between frames. As we can easily try out for ourselves with a flip-book, if we slow down the rate at which the images are presented to our eyes, the retained image will disappear before a new one is in place, and the apparent motion will appear jerky.

However, while appeal to the persistence of vision may explain why we do not see the dark gaps while watching a movie, it does not really offer any account of how the perception of continuous motion comes about. Once the gaps are eliminated, all we have is a seamless succession of images each of which might show a man located at different positions along the street. But how does this give rise to the appearance of smooth motion, both in the cinema as well as in real life (since the same difficulty seems to arise in both cases)?

One possibility often discussed is that our minds "fill in the gaps" between the pictures. This argues that the information we actually receive through the retina is something like the stroboscopic image of the Ping Pong ball taken one shape at a time. Our minds then supply the missing bits at the spatial points where the ball was not observed, thereby smoothing out an essentially discontinuous picture into the smooth parabola produced by the bouncing ball.

Two points make this "filling in" idea very unconvincing. First of all, given that we can split up time very finely (perhaps to an infinite amount) the mind will have to supply quite a large number of images to fill in the gaps. As we noted earlier, the stroboscopic picture of the Ping-Pong ball showed it at forty-seven different positions. In order to come up with anything smooth we would at least need several hundred more. Taking into account that this is a comparatively simple picture, showing just a white ball against a black background, we can imagine the kind of conceptual resources required when having to "smooth out" a more complex motion, like that of a somersaulting gymnast.

Secondly, and more importantly, it is essential to ask *for whose benefit* this smoothing out would be performed. It is not as if we had a little man in our heads watching the world through a retinal projection screen, and our minds, like someone projecting a film in a cinema, had to make sure that the little man did not notice any gaps between the images. Apart from the obvious worry that we would then have to determine how the little man in turn perceived motion, there is simply no place in the brain where all the processing comes together for the benefit of some audience. But if there is no central theater of consciousness there is also no need for our minds to fill in the gaps, since there is no one there to notice them in the first place.

In fact both the appeal to the persistence of vision as well as the notion of "filling in" assume that because it *appears* to us as if we perceived motion in a smooth way there must be a smooth representation somewhere in our perceptual system. It assumes that because the movement of the bouncing Ping-Pong ball does appear to us as continuous, somewhere in our minds there has to be a visual representation of the position of the ball at each point in time. But once we realize that the perception of continuous motion is an illusion based on the perception of discrete frames, this need disappears. Only by taking this illusion too seriously could we think that in order to bring it about all these missing images have to be supplied. This is like thinking that Prince Potemkin, when constructing the facades of illusory houses in the Crimea in order to impress Catherine the Great, also had to construct a fake version of every room within the houses. Our minds can produce the illusion of continuity of motion without there being any continuity in the illusion.

Afterimages, the second ingredient necessary to bring about the illusion of the circle of fire, also give rise to a number of puzzling questions. First of all, afterimages belong to the kind of illusions that cannot be captured in a photograph (unlike, for example, rainbows or mirages). As we saw above afterimages are products of the interaction between our eyes and our brains, and, as cameras have neither eyes nor brains, they do not produce afterimages.

Yet the circle of fire, which we claimed was partly to be explained in terms of afterimages, *can* be photographed. We showed a photograph at the very beginning of this chapter. The circle of fire can be photographed because it *can* be represented on a photograph purely by relying on the motion-blur effect. We have to pick an exposure time that is, as long as it takes for the man to whirl around the torch once in order to get the picture of a full circle. The "exposure time" of the human eye, that is, the time it takes for the brain to put together an image from data obtained via the retina, cannot be manipulated in the same way. A series of afterimages has to be produced as well in order to obtain the desired effect. For this reason the illusory circle of fire we can observe is not quite the same as the circle we can photograph with a camera.

Let us consider a simple example of a negative afterimage. Point a lamp at the image of the Japanese flag below and look straight at it for about thirty seconds. Then look at a blank page. You will observe a half-transparent, round, greenish blob. What kind of thing is this afterimage? There is obviously nothing material colored green out there on the page—you could produce the same effect even if all green objects had miraculously vanished from the world. So could it be something material "in here"? This seems not to be very promising either. You do not have a green disk somewhere in your brain (and it would be quite worrying if you did). We might want to conclude therefore that an afterimage is an *immaterial* object. This would certainly help us in answering the equally difficult question of *where* the afterimage is located. It cannot be on the page, for if you look away from it and direct your eyes at the wall you will see the afterimage there. Equally the afterimage is not on your retina, in your brain, or somewhere in between. But if we agree that the afterimage is immaterial then we would solve that problem, since there is no need for immaterial objects to have a definite location in either space or time (think of the number 2).

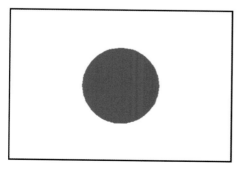

Source of an afterimage

Some might argue that this might be a bit too quick as a refutation of the position that everything that exists is material. Might the afterimage not just be a particular neurophysiological episode in our brains that we interpret *as if* we saw something round and green? Obviously there is no such thing, but this is why afterimages are illusory. However, if we do say this, we have to be able to make sense of the following scenario. Imagine your friend reads this book too, produces the "Japanese flag" afterimage, but claims to see a *blue* dot instead of a green one. This could be because he *really* sees a blue dot, interpreting the neurophysiological episode in a different way than you do. Or he might be suffering from a color *illusion*, mistaking green for blue. For someone arguing that afterimages are neurophysiological episodes there has to be a fact to the matter what the *real appearance* of the dot is to your friend: green or blue. But this seems to be a very peculiar thing to say. How can there be a difference between the afterimage's appearing green or blue, if there is nothing either green or blue involved? There are certainly no light waves of particular frequencies involved here. And how could we possibly find out what the "real appearance" of the dot is to your friend? After all we cannot sneak up into his head and witness him perceiving an afterimage.

This discussion also makes us realize that for all their immaterial fuzziness afterimages seem in some sense to be much more solid than items of the real world. If I see a cup before me there is always the possibility (however remote) that in fact there is no cup there at all. I might be suffering from cup hallucinations, or dreaming, or being deceived by a clever holographic display, and so on. But afterimages appear to be beyond such skeptical worries. If I see an afterimage I have the guarantee there is an afterimage. After all, what would it mean to hallucinate an afterimage? If this just boils down to seeing a green dot where there is none, well, this is just the same as having an afterimage. When dealing with illusory afterimages we seem to have reached solid ground unassailable by skepticism, if only because it appears impossible to distinguish an illusory illusion from a real illusion.

Apart from being immaterial and resistant to skepticism, afterimages might also conceivably be shared. Assume you and your friend first both look at the Japanese flag, then at the same piece of blank paper. Both of you will see a greenish dot more or less at the same place. Are you seeing the same afterimage or two different ones? On the one hand it might seem obvious that you see two different ones: for if both of you look at opposite walls each will see a single green dot on each wall. But then these dots share many of their properties: they are both green, circular, and have the same apparent size. And moreover, why would we think that afterimages behave like ordinary objects, given that they are arguably not material? We might equally interpret the situation by claiming that the afterimage has split and is now simultaneously located on both walls. If we assume that you and your friend are seeing the same afterimage this would entail that they belong to a class of illusions that can be observed by different people—like a mirage, even though, unlike a mirage, they cannot be captured on film.

Returning to the composite illusion of the circle of fire it is interesting to consider the way in which numerous early Buddhist philosophers thought of ordinary objects as illusory in the same way. According to the texts known as the Abhidharma, which present a systematization of a variety of topics implicit in the Buddha's own discourses, the ultimate constituents of the material world are extremely short-lived atomic particles. One set of Abhidharma texts holds that each of these atoms exists only for a moment, only to be replaced by a different atom at the next moment. For this reason medium-sized physical objects are not actually part of the world at all. There is only a huge array of atoms flashing in and out of existence at a rapid pace. The table we experience is a conceptual superimposition on such an array of table-atoms; it is a convenient conceptual fiction that we employ for getting around in the world. According to this cinematographic view of reality a table is actually not very different from the illusory circle of fire. In the same way that there is no circle out there, but merely a succession of points of light at different successive places from which our minds then construct a circle of fire based on the somewhat complex visual phenomena examined above, there is no table in the world either. Both the circle of fire and the table are illusions superimposed on a more fundamental reality.

It is interesting to note that the authors of the Abhidharma had quite precise ideas about the length of these fundamental moments. They specify the length of several phenomena in terms of moments: a finger snap is supposed to take sixty moments, a thought ninety moments, there are 4,500 moments in a minute, and 3,240,000 in a day. One moment therefore lasts about thirteen milliseconds. This appears to be quite a good estimate of the duration of the smallest units of *subjective time*, that is of the shortest duration two

Abhidharma manuscript

events have to be apart so that we can still experience them as two events. This duration depends on the sensory modality in which the event is presented to us—for example, human beings can distinguish auditory events most finely. To experience two sounds as distinct they have to be at least ten milliseconds apart, which roughly corresponds to one moment in the Abhidharma sense.

Objective time (if such a thing exists) can of course be divided into moments of much smaller durations. Currently the shortest duration measured is on the attosecond scale (one attosecond is 10^{-18} seconds). Whether there are any absolutely shortest durations or "temporal atoms" is an open question. A potential candidate is the Planck unit, the time it would take for a photon to travel across a Planck length (about 10^{-20} of the diameter of a proton) at the speed of light. The Planck unit is a very short duration indeed: it takes 10^{26} Planck units to make up one attosecond.

Interestingly enough what we experience as "the present moment" is considerably longer than the smallest unit of subjective time. Various psychological experiments succeeded in demonstrating that the duration of the present moment is about two to three seconds. For example, if we listen to the continuous clack-clack of a metronome it is possible to give a subjective accent to every second beat (clack **clack** clack **clack** clack . . .)—as long as the "clacks" are not more than three seconds apart. Events separated by longer durations cannot be grouped into a single temporal unit anymore.

The creation of the present moment is a sophisticated fabrication employed by the brain to deal with the fact that different pieces of information belonging together arrive at the brain at different times. If someone touches my foot, this tactile information has a longer way to travel before it reaches the brain than if someone touches my nose. Moreover, different kinds of information are processed in the brain with different speeds; sounds are processed very quickly, visual information takes a much longer time. Our brains deal with this temporal chaos by creating an illusory present, such that all information arriving within this time-window of two or three seconds is regarded as simultaneous. Even the present moment, which seems to be the "most real" time there is and the most direct contact we can make with the world turns out to be, as the authors of the Abhidharma would put it, a superimposition on the rapid flow of moments flashing in and out of existence.

If we accept the Abhidharma account, which sees all phenomena as similar to the illusory circle of fire, we end up with a two-level view of the world. On the one hand there are the illusory medium-sized objects, tables and chairs, Catherine wheels and so forth, while on the other hand there is the rock-bottom layer of reality that is composed of the momentary and short-lived particles. The particles are real while everything else is an illusory conceptual superimposition.

This view was severely criticized by a variety of later Buddhist authors who saw problems with treating the momentary particles as the foundational level of reality. A criticism formulated by the Madhyamaka school going back to the second-century Indian philosopher Nāgārjuna runs as follows: we think of the Abhidharma moments as produced—one moment brings about the next, which then causes the succeeding one and so forth. But causation between moments, the critics claimed, is something in the mind, not something out there in the world. For when we postulate that a present moment causes a future moment, the future moment is only something supplied by our minds or our expectations. When the present moment exists the future moment does not yet do so, so there cannot be a relation connecting the two, as this would require two existent objects that it could relate. But if the notion of a moment now turns out to involve the notion of causality at an essential point, and if the notion of causality is a conceptual construct, moments cannot escape the charge of being conceptual constructs either. And since whatever is a conceptual construct is mind-dependent to some extent, moments cannot be the rock-bottom of reality. They, like everything else, are an artifice of the mind.

Depending on whether we accept this argument, we therefore have two different ways of interpreting the statement that all phenomena are like the illusory wheel of fire. We can either see them as a fictitious superimposition on a real basis, or as an illusory phenomenon founded on something that, in turn, is just as illusory.

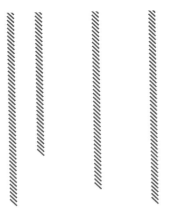

RAINBOWS

འཇའ་ཚོན་

TIBETAN RAINBOWS—or at least the rainbows depicted in Tibetan art—have the curious property of not being bows at all. Streams of rainbow light rarely appear in the shape of the familiar arc but can be seen to take all sorts of forms: curling up to heaven like multicolored incense smoke, radiating from Buddha's funeral pyre, their colored bands interlaced with thin strips of gold, or forming transparent rainbow-orbs floating in the sky.

The sacred associations of the rainbow are scattered across the world's mythology, as the sign of the covenant in the book of Genesis, Indra's bow, or Ishtar's necklace, and the Tibetan view of the rainbow is no exception. The sight of the rainbow is always seen as a good omen, and generally as one of high religious significance. In the biography of the eleventh-and twelfth-century Tibetan saint Milarepa (མི་ལ་རས་པ་) we find the following account of his cremation:

> Then the funeral pyre appeared as a palace made of rainbow-light, of rectangular shape, with four gates and ornamented archways. Above this hovered canopies and umbrellas, also made of rainbow light. . . . In the smoke the sweet smell of incense arose and within this billowing shroud a multitude of clouds of offering, with parasols, victory banners and so forth were seen, all made of rainbow light.

This view of rainbows as fairly flexible and not necessarily bow-shaped objects goes back well into pre-Buddhist Tibetan history, when a vertical rainbow was of particular importance. According to Tibetan historiography there are no tombs of any of the first seven kings of Tibet, since they left no corpse on Earth. Descended from heaven they continued to be connected to their celestial place of origin by a rainbow cord (རྨུ་ཐག་) by means of which they would rejoin their ancestors once they had passed their time

Buddha's cremation

on Earth. For this reason the ancient Tibetan kings were also referred to by the term *ten wa* (འཐེན་བ་), which literally means "one who is pulled up." The eighth king, Drigum Tsänpo (གྲི་གུམ་བཙན་པོ་), was the first one to leave behind a corpse (and thus a grave) because an evil minister tricked him into whirling a sword above his head, thereby cutting the rainbow cord.

It is hard to overlook the continuity of the ascent along the heavenly cord, leaving the body "to melt away like a rainbow" and a particularly interesting, uniquely Tibetan contribution to the plethora of sacred rainbow phenomena. This is the concept of a *ja lü* (འཇའ་ལུས་) or rainbow body. The idea is that at the death of a highly accomplished Buddhist practitioner no earthly corpse will remain, but that the body is rather gradually dissolved into rainbow light, leaving behind only the clothes and, interestingly, the hair and the nails. The concept of a rainbow body is associated particularly with a set of teachings called *dzog chen* (རྫོགས་ཆེན་) or Great Perfection, and among these specifically with the practice of *trek chö* (ཁྲེགས་ཆོད་), the "cutting through" of illusion. This practice, which, if successful, is supposed to allow the meditator to dissolve his body into light, is mainly found in the Nyingma (རྙིང་མ་) and Kargyü (བཀའ་བརྒྱུད་) schools of Tibetan Buddhism.[41]

In recent times there have been claims about the dissolution into a rainbow body having actually been caught on film. The second of the two pictures (opposite) of the XVIth Karmapa, head of the Kargyü school, is said to have been taken during a religious ceremony at his monastic seat in Sikkim in 1980, one year before his death. In this picture his body appears almost transparent, so that it is possible to make out the mythological animals on the brocade draping behind him (a Chinese mythical beast called *qilin*, having the body of a deer, the tail of an ox, horse's hooves, the scales of a dragon, and a single horn). Regardless of whether we consider this photograph to be a fabrication or not it seems clear that the phenomenon it is supposed to show is quite different from the rainbow body as usually conceived. If only the body (minus the hair and nails) disappears we would expect to see something more like the drawing in the following figure, where the person on the throne gradually disappears, leaving his robes

---

41. The Nyingma school constitutes the oldest school of Tibetan Buddhism and dates back to the times of the first transmission of the Buddhist teachings to Tibet from India in the eighth and ninth centuries. A central figure of the Nyingma school is the "lotus born" Padmasambhava, affectionately referred to by the Tibetans as *Guru Rinpoche* (གུ་རུ་རིན་པོ་ཆེ་), the "Precious Teacher." He is well known for his conversion of malevolent indigenous Tibetan spirits. The Kargyü school traces its beginnings back to tenth-century India. Three of its Tibetan masters, Milarepa (མི་ལ་རས་པ་), together with his teacher Marpa (མར་པ་) and his disciple Gampopa (སྒམ་པོ་པ་), proved to be particularly important for the development of Buddhism in Tibet.

Two Photographs of the XVIth Karmapa

Traditional depiction of a rainbow body

behind, rather than a fully dressed man becoming more and more translucent.

In any case, a less obscure but equally interesting rainbow phenomenon that captured the Tibetan imagination is the circular rainbow. While most of the rainbows we see have the form of an arc, the ends of rainbows found in many Tibetan scrolls or *thangka* paintings meet to form a circle hovering in the sky, often enclosing the figure of a saint or Buddha seated within it, resting in empty space.[42]

---

42. Occasionally the circular rainbow can also be rectangular. Tibetan scrolls are displayed in often very intricate brocade mountings. The painting itself is always surrounded by two narrow bands of colored brocade, an inner red one and an outer yellow one. These bands are called the "red" and "yellow" rainbow, respectively (འཇའ་དམར་འཇའ་སེར་) and constitute a stylized rainbow framing of the entire painting. It might therefore not be unjustified to claim that *every* properly displayed Tibetan sacred painting is presented as surrounded by a glory of rainbow light.

Although most people have presumably seen several rainbows over the course of their lives, sightings of circular rainbows are comparatively rare. Nevertheless, as a matter of principle circular rainbows are not any more rare than the conventional arc-shaped rainbows, as every rainbow is by nature circular. To understand why this is so it is instructive to look a bit more closely at how a rainbow is formed.

The key concept for understanding how a rainbow comes about is the refraction of light. "Refraction" means that a wave (a light wave, or any other sort of wave) changes its direction when traveling from one medium to another. Typical examples of refraction occur when a light wave first travels through air, and then enters a piece of glass, or a drop of water. The change in direction is caused by a change of speed, which is in turn due to the different molecular structure of the medium in which light travels. When traveling through glass, for example, light only travels with about two-thirds of its speed in air.

We can see how the change in speed will cause a change in direction

by looking at the simple example of a ceremonial procession carrying a shrine. Let us suppose that the shrine is carried cross-country, and at some point in time the procession has to cross a muddy field, where the carriers have to go more slowly. Now whenever a row of shrine-carriers starts to cross the line into the field, the man on the left will be slowed down first. He will thus get a little bit behind the rest of the row. Some moments later the man to his right will also enter the field and will also fall behind a bit. After half the men have passed into the field the

Maitreya seated in a circular rainbow

initially straight first row will now be slightly bent, pointing forward. After the whole procession has entered the field the rows will be straightened out again, but they are now parallel with the upper bit of the pointed row, rather than the lower bit. The direction of the whole procession has changed by traveling from a medium in which the carriers can move faster (the road) into one in which they move more slowly (the field). The very same thing

Matsuri procession

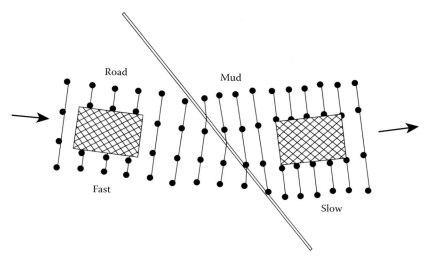

Progress of a procession

happens to a ray of light entering a piece of glass or a jar of water at an oblique angle. That is the reason why an oar will look bent in water.

What we need for understanding how a rainbow is formed, however, is not just an account of how light can change direction, but also how it is split up into different colors. This dispersion of light can be easily derived from the notion of refraction by taking into account that the ordinary white light we perceive is actually a variety of different wavelengths traveling together. Light of different wavelengths is perceived as having different colors. If light is not in a vacuum its different wavelengths travel at different speeds; violet light travels comparatively slowly, while red light travels much faster. If we now imagine that some of the people carrying the shrine are better at walking in the mud than others and are therefore a lot faster, it is clear what would happen to the procession. Different groups of carriers would walk into different parts of the muddy field, the group would get dispersed, and the shrine would end up lying somewhere in the middle. The same picture (without the stranded shrine) emerges in the case of a beam of light entering a piece of glass at an angle. The different wavelengths unified in the white light will travel at different speeds in the glass and get split up into different colors, depending on their speed. If the back of the piece of glass is not parallel with the front (as, for example, in a prism) the effect will not be reversed, and light will leave the glass in this dispersed state, the different strands of light having been unwoven into the colors of a rainbow.

In order to see a rainbow we have to have the sun at our back and drops of water (rain, or the spray caused by a fountain or waterfall) in front of us. As a ray of light enters a drop of water it is bent and broken up into different colors. The back of the raindrop functions like a mirror, so each of the various, now distinct rays is reflected and bent once again as it leaves the drop and travels back to our eyes. Light of different colors leaves the drop at different angles relative to the incoming beam of light: red light comes out at an angle of 42°, blue light at 40.6°, and all the other colors at angles in between.

If we trace an imaginary line from the sun behind our heads, through our eyes, and further on we reach the antisolar point, which is exactly opposite the sun. If the sun is high up in the sky the antisolar point is below the horizon, or if it is just setting, above the horizon. This imaginary antisolar line will go through the center of the rainbow that is yet to form. Since the antisolar line and the rays of sunlight are parallel, the light leaving a drop of rain at 42° will be seen at 42° up from this imaginary line. We can imagine two cones stacked into one another, with their apex at the center of one of our eyes, a bigger one, 42° from the antisolar line, and a smaller one, at 40.6°. Between these two cones, the rainbow will be observed; the bigger circle will mark the edge of red light, the smaller one the edge of blue light.

Because of this fact, all rainbows are in fact circular, rather than segments of an arc. The reason why we usually only see the segments is because something gets in the way, the ground, the side of a mountain, or a bank of clouds. One might want to argue that in a very mountainous region such as Tibet the whole circle of a rainbow is observed more easily than elsewhere, so that its presence in Tibetan art could be explained in this way. Just standing on top of a mountain, however, does not help a great deal if we want to observe a circular rainbow. Since the sun must be behind us, the lower half of the rainbow will invariably be blocked by the mountain's shadow. Nevertheless, a region that varies a lot in height provides us with a better chance of seeing circular rainbows than more horizontal landscapes would. One way of doing this is by looking down a deep abyss, with the sun overhead, toward an agglomeration of raindrops lower down in the valley. A miniature version of this can be produced in our own backyard on a sunny day by employing a garden hose. When the sun is high up in the sky, produce a fine spray of water with the hose, then look downward into the watery mist. You will see a small but perfectly circular rainbow. Like in the case of the mountain view, however, your shadow is likely to get into the way.

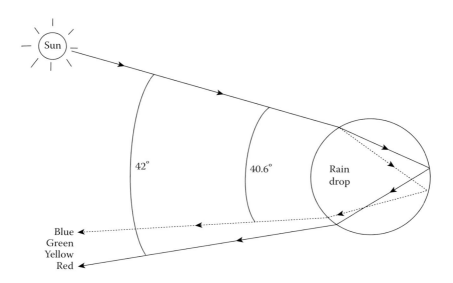

Refraction of light in a drop of water

Why is a rainbow an example of illusion? It is an excellent illustration of an object that does not exist in the way in which it appears to exist. First of all, consider the location of a rainbow. When we see a bridge crossing a river in the distance, we observe that the abutments supporting the arches touch the water or the land at specific points. If we go near enough we can touch the very spot of the bridge's foundation, walk around it, and mark its place on a map.

If we try to do the same with the places where the arc of a rainbow touches the ground we have to prepare ourselves for a disappointment. It *seems* as if the ends of the rainbow mark two precise spots. Yet when we actually try to determine the precise location of these we realize that the trick cannot be done. As soon as we are close enough to the spot in question the rainbow just disappears. This impossibility of determining the exact place where a rainbow touches down makes it possible to promise a pot of gold (or a wish-fulfilling gem in the Indian tradition) to those who succeed in doing so.

This is a rather curious fact. Nobody is surprised that it is impossible to find the location of the imaginary city you dreamt about last night. Similarly, suppose you look straight into the light of your desk lamp, thereby creating the hovering afterimage of a bright, colored spot. Now to ask where in front of you the spot is seems like a silly question. This is because dreams and afterimages are usually regarded as private objects: they exist only in your mind and are only ever seen by a single observer, namely you. They are also mind-dependent: in a world of dead matter, without minds there would be no afterimages, and no dreams either.

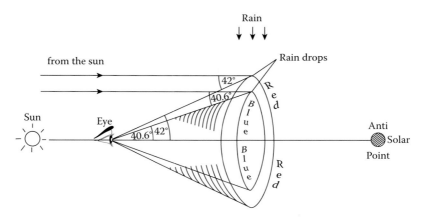

Rainbow cone

But a rainbow is not like this. It is not private: a group of people can see a rainbow at the same time, a rainbow can be photographed, or filmed. None of this can be done with dreams or afterimages. There are no devices for recording dreams, nor is it possible to photograph the visual image you see with your mind's eye. Nor is a rainbow mind-dependent: light would still be refracted by drops of water in exactly the same way if human beings did not exist. So why is it that a rainbow, a publicly observable, material object that exists independently of our minds, does not have a fixed location?

As was noted earlier, the rainbow you observe is constituted by the reflected light of water drops hovering in the air that intersect two cones stacked into one another, both of which have their apex at the place of your eye. To make things simpler, assume you have a powerful searchlight placed where your eye is, which projects a cone of light into the far distance. If some hovering mists intersect with the cone, you see the circular spot of light in the mists. In this situation it is clear that as you move, the spot of light will change. If you move to the right, so will the spot. If you move closer it will decrease in size, if you retreat it will grow larger. The moment you move to measure the size of the spot projected or to determine its precise location it will move and change, staying forever elusive.

Furthermore, somebody with a similar searchlight standing next to you will project a spot similar to yours, but distinct from it. If we apply this last fact back to the case of the rainbow, it becomes apparent that when you and your friend both observe a rainbow, both of you see a distinct object. *Your* rainbow is the intersection of the drops of water with the cones beginning at *your* eye, your friend's rainbow is the intersection with the cone beginning at *his*. It is therefore never possible for two people to observe the same rainbow. Each of you observe a distinct object, and even though these objects might partially overlap, they are quite distinct. There is no unique rainbow involved in this situation, anymore than a case in which two people simultaneously dream of missing a bus involves a unique bus.

The nineteenth-century English poet Gerald Manley Hopkins summed this up well in a poem without a title:

The rainbow shines, but only in the thought
Of him that looks. Yet not in that alone,
For who makes rainbows by invention?
And many standing round a waterfall

See one bow each, yet not the same to all,
But each a hand's breadth further than the next.
The sun on falling water writes the text
Which yet is in the eye or in the thought.

But we might think we have gone too far. After all, that a spot changes as you approach does not mean it has no location; otherwise you would also want to say that the elusive fly you try to catch has no location either. It has a location, but a variable one. Similarly, is not saying that each man only ever sees his own rainbow denying that rainbows are public phenomena, unlike dreams and afterimages, as we concluded earlier?

Consider the Chinese tea bowl standing on my desk in front of me. We might want to argue that far from being an elusive, locationless, and observer-dependent phenomenon the rainbow is in fact pretty much an ordinary object like the bowl. First of all, the fact that a rainbow's location depends on our location does not mean it has no location at all. The searchlight produces a spot of light with definite boundaries in the mists—it just happens to change when we move the light. The difficulty of determining where the ends of a rainbow touch the ground is a purely practical one. Of course we cannot do this ourselves, for as soon as we move, the rainbow does too. But we could for example send out a small expedition of men carrying flags or banners mounted on sticks. We could then direct these men (by means of a megaphone, or with some other suitable device) to where we see the rainbow touching the earth— all the time being careful not to move our heads. After they have planted the flags in the ground we could go there, and start digging for the hidden treasure.

Similarly it is incorrect to say that my friend and I each see a different rainbow. The yellow bowl in front of me shows orchids and rocks on the one side, and a delicately inscribed poem on the other. Now from where I am sitting I can see the rocks and the orchids, but not the poem. You, however, sitting opposite me, can see the poem, but not the rocks and the orchids. But we would hardly want to infer from this that *each of us was seeing a different bowl*, one with a painting for me, one with a poem for you. Obviously what we see is the same bowl from two different perspectives. Similarly, my friend and I do not see two different rainbows; we see the same rainbow from two different points of view.

But if we consider the matter a bit more closely it becomes clear that treating rainbows as if they were ordinary objects leads to strange results.

One thing that distinguishes the tea bowl from the rainbow is that the bowl has its location independently of me. If I move the bowl does not move with me. Of course the bowl has moved *relative* to me (which is the same as me having moved relative to the bowl), but relative to all the other things in my study (the desk, the bookshelves, the stacks of paper) the bowl remains stationary. A rainbow, however, moves with its observer. If I try to direct my little expedition of flag bearers to the end of my rainbow while moving myself, they will never get there. If I did the same thing with an ordinary object like a bridge there would be no problem, since even as I move, the bridge will stay where it is. It therefore becomes clear that while it is misleading to say that a rainbow has *no* location in space (because there are some scenarios, like the one described above, where its location relative to a static observer could be fixed), it is equally misleading to treat it in the same manner as the tea bowl in front of me (because the bowl will not wander across my desk when I move, while the rainbow will move across the landscape when I change my position).

Secondly, consider the question of whether two people can ever see the same rainbow. In the case of the tea bowl it is obvious that it can be observed from different perspectives, and that different observers are likely to disagree about certain aspects of what they see: I see the painted side of the bowl, you the side with the calligraphy; I see it two feet away from me, for you it is one foot closer. They do not, however, disagree about where the bowl is located relative to other stationary objects like the desk it stands on. But this is precisely what happens in the case of rainbows. If we imagined that the tea bowl behaved like a rainbow, strange things would happen. Imagine the bowl stands on the desk between us. Both of us get up to lift the bowl. Rather than taking hold of the same object we will end up bumping into one another, holding nothing at all in our hands. Our respective bowls have moved to other parts of the room, since they have moved with us, and are exactly as far away as they were in the beginning. It appears now that it hardly makes sense to consider the situation in which we both see a rainbow as one in which a single object—namely the rainbow—is seen by both of us. If this was the case we should at least be able to agree on *where* this object is, relative to other unmoved parts of the landscape. But since the location of the rainbow we see depends on where *we* are, such agreement is impossible.

Rainbows are illusory objects if we assume that they behave in the same way as ordinary things, like tea bowls and bridges. A rainbow changes its position as we move, so we cannot get any closer to it. Nor is there a single rainbow two different people observe. The two objects share sufficiently many properties to make it convenient to identify them for many purposes. But if we investigate the light of the rainbow in the light of reason it becomes apparent that this identification is mistaken.

Rainbows are not inherently illusory, however. What is illusory, and what not, depends on our expectations about how things should behave. If there were more rainbow-like objects around, bridges and tea bowls might be considered to be the ones with the bizarre properties, since they stay where they are if we move toward them, and since different people can reach an agreement about their location. To this extent rainbows are only illusory because they constitute a minority when compared to all the other kinds of things observed in the world.

LIGHTNING

གློག

THE TIBETAN tradition—like most Oriental cultures—associates both light-ning and thunder with the dragon. Indeed the Tibetan term *druk* (འབྲུག་) means both "thunder" and "dragon"; *druk kä* (འབྲུག་སྐད་), "the dragon's language," is another term for the clap of thunder. A well-known lineage of Tibetan Bud-dhism, the Drukpa Kargyü (འབྲུག་པ་བཀའ་བརྒྱུད་), bears the dragon in its name. When its founder, Tsangpa Gyare,[43] arrived at the place where the future Namdruk Gompa (གནམ་འབྲུག་དགོན་པ་), the Monastery of the Celestial Dragon,[44] was to be built, he saw nine[45] dragons roaring up in the sky amid claps of thunder, producing, miraculously and somewhat incongruously, a rain of white flowers.

In commemoration of this auspicious apparition of the nine dragons (which were taken to be manifestations of nine Indian saints or *mahasid-dhas*), Tsangpa Gyare named his newly established lineage Drukpa Kargyü, the Oral Tradition of the Dragon. A disciple of Tsangpa Gyare later converted

---

43. འགྲོ་བའི་མགོན་པོ་གཙང་པ་རྒྱ་རས་ཡེ་ཤེས་རྡོ་རྗེ་ (1161–1211). As the first head of the Drukpa Kargyü school, Tsangpa Gyare is regarded as the first Gyalwang Drukpa (རྒྱལ་དབང་འབྲུག་པ་); his present reincarnation is the twelfth bearer of that title.

44. Namdruk Monastery (འབྲུག་ཆེན་བྱང་ཆུབ་ཆོས་གླིང་), founded in 1206, is located about 19 miles southwest of Lhasa and was completely destroyed during the Cultural Revolution. Attempts at reconstructing a small number of buildings began in 1986.

45. These might have been the nine varieties of dragon distinguished in Chinese mythology: the celestial dragons (天龍), who guard the heavenly palaces; the spiritual dragons (神龍), who control wind and rain; the dragons of hidden treasures (伏藏龍), who cause volcanoes to erupt; the underground dragons (地龍); the winged dragon (應龍); the oldest of all of them and servant of the Yellow Emperor; the horned dragons (蛟龍); the coiling dragons (蟠龍), who inhabit lakes; the yellow dragon (黃龍), who revealed the trigrams to Fu Hsi; and finally the dragon kings (龍王), who dwell in the crystal palaces. Dragons have a strong con-nection with the number nine. They are taken to have eighty-one (9×9) scales and are described in terms of nine likenesses: they have a head like a camel, horns like a deer, eyes like a hare, a neck like a snake, scales like a carp, ears like a bull, a belly like a frog, paws like a tiger, and claws like an eagle. The standard Chinese court dress during the Qing dynasty was a brocade robe decorated with nine dragons, three on the front and back, two on the shoulders and one "hidden dragon" on the inside of the flap.

Tsangpa Gyare (top row, middle)

the valleys of western Bhutan and established the Drukpa Kargyü as the dominant transmission there, which it remains to this day. To the Bhutanese, Bhutan is known as *druk yül* (འབྲུག་ཡུལ་), the Land of the Dragon.

Chinese iconography often depicts dragons as fighting over a large celestial pearl floating in the sky. Contact with the pearl causes the lightning flash, which outlines the shape of the dragon, while its accompanying roar is the sound of the thunder.

In the depiction from a Tibetan scroll painting on page 138, however, the streaks of lightning are seen to be issuing directly from the dragon's mouth.

The physical basis of lightning is surprisingly complex, and some aspects of it (such as the exact way in which clouds are electrically charged) are not yet completely understood. In a very general way we can conceive of lightning as an electric discharge occurring between the lower, negatively charged part of a cloud, and the positively charged surface of the earth. (However, lightning can also take place between clouds or within a cloud.) One explanation for this charge separation between the different parts of the cloud is that the water droplets that make up rising moisture collide on their way up with droplets frozen to ice crystals, which move downward. By these collisions electrons are knocked off the droplets and accumulate in the lower parts of the cloud. The droplets that have just lost an electron and are now positively charged accumulate in the upper part of the cloud. Once the charge difference between the negatively charged lower part of the cloud and the positively charged surface of the earth becomes strong enough, lightning strikes.

The electric energy discharged at this time generates immense heat. The temperature along the channel of lightning is about 54,000°F (by comparison, the temperature of the surface of the sun is about 9,000°F). The air in

the vicinity of this channel heats up rapidly and expands, producing a series of waves that we hear as thunder.

The existence of thunder is what makes lightning an example of illusion. This is because even though lightning (the spark jumping) and thunder (the air being heated up around it) are a single event, we experience two events separated by a temporal gap: first we see the flash of lightning and after some time we hear the sound of the thunder. This difference between the apparent and the real

A dragon with flaming pearl

temporal order of thunder and lightning is easily explained by the different transmission speeds of sound and light. Sound travels at a rate of about 1,000 feet per second in air, light at 186,000 miles per second in a vacuum—about a million times faster. It is thus not surprising that the light of the discharge that constitutes the lightning reaches our eyes virtually at the same time it strikes, but the sound of the thunder travels only one-fifth of a mile in a single second.

The relation of lightning and thunder is an example of the discrepancy between the objective ordering of events (the sequence in which events follow one another "out there") and their subjective ordering (the way in which their perceptions follow one another "in here"). We usually think that these two line up perfectly: if the dropping of the porcelain tea cup precedes its shattering on the floor, our *perception* of dropping it will precede our perception of it shattering as well. Conversely, if a *perception* of an event precedes another one we assume that the events of which they are perceptions are related in the same way. The event that is perceived first comes before the one that is perceived second.

However, the simple example of lightning and thunder demonstrates that

Tibetan dragon producing lightning.

this naive view of the lineup of objective and subjective ordering of events cannot be correct. According to the objective ordering of time, thunder and lightning are simultaneous. This, however, is not true for their subjective ordering in perception: there the lightning is seen first and then, after an interval, the thunder is heard. Our perception of events in this case is an illusion because the way their sequence *appears* to us differs from the way it really *is*. We would be mistaken if we assumed a perfect lineup

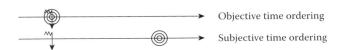

An objective and subjective sequence of two events

between subjective and objective order and if we thought that the clap of thunder happened some time after lightning, rather than at the same time. The subjective ordering of our perceptions is not always a good guide to the objective temporal ordering of the things perceived.

This fact was illustrated by a variety of psychological experiments conducted at the beginning of the twentieth century, most notably by the German psychologist Wilhelm Wundt. He investigated a variety of temporal illusions, including those concerning the perception of the *duration* of an event, as well as concerning the *ordering* of series of events. One device employed for getting a better understanding of the second kind of illusion is the so-called complication clock.

This device consists of a dial divided into sections like a clock face, and a single pointer. The clock could be set up in such a way that a bell would sound when the pointer reached a certain position. The subject of the experiment is asked to watch the moving pointer and say where the pointer is when the bell sounds. His task is therefore to determine the temporal relation between a series of visual perceptions (pointer at 14, at 14½, at 15, etc.) and an auditory perception (the sound of the bell).

Now let us suppose the clock is set up in such a way that the bell sounds when the counter hits position 15. In this case the two events "pointer at 15" and "bell sounding" are objectively simultaneous, that is they happen at the same time in the objective ordering of events, just like lightning and thunder. Now we might expect that this is not what is in fact perceived, but that the subject rather claims that the bell sounds when the pointer reaches, say, position 15½. Unlike in the case of lightning the explanation of this would not have to be sought in the different velocities of light and sound, but rather in the fact that after hearing the sound of the bell

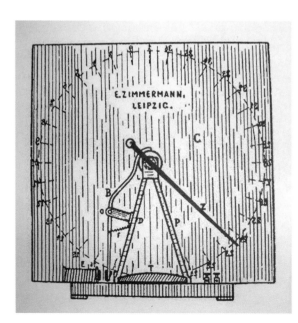

A complication clock

the subject has to check where the pointer is at that moment. In the short moment it takes for him to react the pointer has already moved a bit, so that the first position of the pointer perceived after the sound of the bell, and later regarded as coinciding with it, is not where the pointer really was when the bell sounded, but a bit further along the dial.

Wundt referred to this phenomenon as *positive time-displacement*. Here some stimulus is regarded as simultaneous with an event that happens a bit later than it. Now an interesting fact about Wundt's experiments is that far more frequent than the cases of *positive time-displacement* or indeed cases of a correct identification of the pointer position, which involved no time-displacement at all, were cases of *negative time-displacement*. In these cases the sound of the bell was associated with an *earlier* position on the dial, for example with position 14½ rather than with 15.

Now this is a very peculiar result. To see why, consider a different setup. Assume there is a machine spitting out tennis balls in rapid succession.

For each ball leaving the machine there is a click. You are told that once in a while the click will be replaced by the sound of a bell; you are then supposed to catch the ball leaving the machine at that moment. Now it is clear that if your reaction is a bit too slow you might not catch the ball associated with the bell, but only a later one. Suppose ball number five is leaving the machine when the bell sounds, but you only catch ball number six. This would correspond to positive time-displacement. But now consider the equivalent of negative time-displacement. You would catch ball number four, even though the bell only sounds at ball number five. But assuming that you do not randomly catch balls, and also do not clairvoyantly

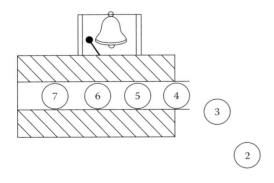

The ball-throwing machine

know when the ball is going to come, how are you going to catch a ball *before* the signal sounds?

Wundt tried to explain negative time-displacement by arguing that the entire sequence of visual impressions (of the pointer at various positions on the dial) is present in consciousness and that the auditory impression of the sound of the bell that enters consciousness has to be associated with a particular one: either with the impression of the pointer position that was really simultaneous with the sound, or with an earlier or later one. According to Wundt, the more our attention is focused on a particular impression, the earlier it is placed in the temporal sequence. Negative temporal displacement is therefore a result of placing particular anticipatory attention on the sound of the bell that is about to happen.

Now the peculiar feature of this explanation is that on this understanding the simultaneity of two events entering our senses is not automatically reflected in a perception of these events which are regarded as simultaneous. It rather seems that depending on where our attention is focused the perceptions of two objectively simultaneous events can happen to have any order in consciousness. To this extent the ball-throwing machine just described is only an imperfect model of how our perception of events works, since in this model we can never catch a ball associated with the bell before the bell sounds. But we apparently can associate the 14½ position with the sound of the bell even if it only sounds at 15. In the analogous case we would therefore somehow have to be able, after catching a ball more or less at random, to *make* the sound of the bell coincide with its leaving the machine. It is as if both the visual sequence of balls leaving the machine and the auditory sequence of clicks and the bell are floating around independently in our consciousness and can be moved against one another so that more or less any part of the visual sequence (such as ball number four leaving the machine) can be aligned with another part of the auditory sequence (such the bell sounding).

In a similar way we would be able to match the visual sequence of the different positions of the pointer and the auditory sequence of silences interrupted by the sound of the bell in such a way that the sound is made to coincide with the different pointer positions at 14½, 15, 15½, and so forth.

It therefore becomes evident that at least regarding events following in relatively quick succession, their perceived sequence is not always a good guide to their actual sequence, nor does the actual sequence give us a reliable indication of the order in which the events will be perceived. In cases like

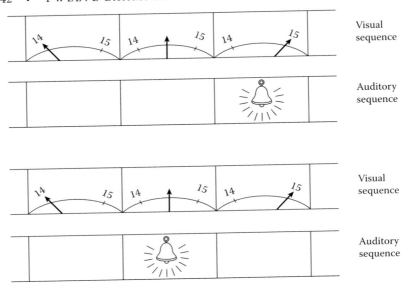

Two ways of lining up visual and auditory sequences

these in which the objective and subjective sequence of events are incongruous we are subject to a temporal illusion.

A series of curious and controversial experiments on the temporal ordering of experience became possible once direct interaction with the brain of a locally anesthetized but fully conscious subject could be achieved. Such operations are sometimes performed when brain tissue is removed during the treatment of epilepsy. The surgeon will stimulate particular parts of the cortex with a weak electric current and ask the patient what he experiences. In this way removing any parts that are absolutely vital can be avoided.

A phenomenon encountered during experiments conducted by the neuroscientist Benjamin Libet in the 1960s is the so-called masking. The setup is very simple.

First the patient's skin is stimulated, for example by touch. This impulse then travels upward through the nervous system until it reaches the brain. This journey takes about ten to twenty milliseconds.[46] After some time in the brain this neurophysiological stimulus finally enters experience: we feel that someone has touched our hand. Libet now determined that if a specific region of the cortex is stimulated by an electric current up to five hundred

---

46. This is quite fast. To give the reader an idea of the orders of magnitude involved here: the flap of a honeybee's wing lasts for about five milliseconds, a blink of an eye for one hundred milliseconds, uttering a single syllable takes about two hundred milliseconds (so saying "A-B-C-D-E" takes about one second).

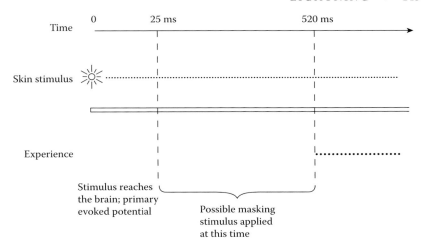

The masking phenomenon

milliseconds after the skin stimulus has reached the brain, nothing is experienced at all. The section under the double line in the above diagram would remain blank: the masking stimulus somehow managed to "waylay" the skin stimulus on its way to conscious experience.

This fact has an interesting consequence. Since the "waylaying" of the skin stimulus could happen up to five hundred milliseconds after the stimulus reached the brain, it could obviously not have entered consciousness any earlier (as one cannot intercept somebody who has already arrived). The stimulus needs a time of continued "reverberation" in the brain of up to five hundred milliseconds in order to achieve "neuronal adequacy." But this seems to mean that our perception of the world always lags half a second behind the objective timing of events, since it may take this much time for consciousness to build up. This, however, would be extremely puzzling. Not only are we not aware of such an ubiquitous delay, but human reaction times can be much shorter than half a second (in some cases as little as two hundred milliseconds).

Libet tried to account for the lack of any time lag in our perception of the world by introducing the peculiar notion of "backwards referral in time." Here the idea is that our brains somehow manage to antedate the onset of experience of the skin stimulus so that it does not happen five hundred milliseconds after the stimulus reached the brain but roughly at the same time, that is, at the time of the "primary evoked potential."

This backwards referral in time can be seen at work in a different, slightly more complex experiment. One of the interesting facts about

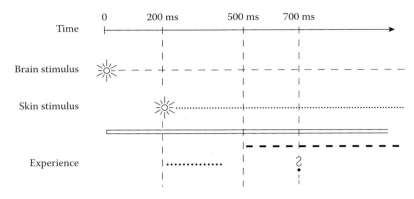

An experiment with temporal order

being able to access the brain of a conscious patient directly is that certain sensations can be caused by direct stimulation of different parts of the cortex that give rise to sensations like those commonly processed in these parts of the brain. For example, by stimulating a part of the somatosensory cortex it is possible to create a sensation very much like a skin sensation, which nevertheless feels qualitatively different. This is what Libet did in his second experiment. First the brain of the patient was stimulated directly, then, about two hundred milliseconds later, his skin was stimulated as well. The patient was then asked which of the two sensations came first.

Regarding the brain stimulus (represented by a broken line) everything goes as we would expect. After a period of five hundred milliseconds it reaches neuronal adequacy and subsequently enters consciousness. But the skin stimulus (represented by dots) does not do what we might think it would. Given that it was started at two hundred milliseconds we would expect it to be felt after an additional five hundred, that is, at the place of the question mark, at about seven hundred milliseconds. However, the strange fact is that the skin stimulus is actually felt at about two hundred milliseconds, right after the stimulation of the skin and *before the brain stimulus*! What happens here is a complete inversion of the time ordering in the brain and in the consciousness. If we look at the brain from the outside, the objective sequence of events is brain stimulus—skin stimulus. But the subjective order of experience is just the reverse: skin stimulus—brain stimulus.

Now this curious result is accounted for by Libet's assumed referral backward in time. The experience of the skin stimulus is referred backward from the point where we would expect it (at seven hundred milliseconds) to an earlier place at about two hundred milliseconds, the time of the primary evoked potential, when the stimulus entered the brain. But the direct stimulation of the brain, entering the brain in a nonstandard way, is not referred backward and is thus experienced only after a time delay of half a second. For this reason the objective order of events is subjectively reversed.

Libet's experiment provides us with an example of a temporal illusion that is similar to that of lightning and thunder, but at the same time more fundamental. In both cases there is a discrepancy between the objective and subjective ordering of events. The present discrepancy, however, cannot be accounted for in terms of different transmission speeds of the events involved. Something more complex is going on here.

The most radical consequence drawn from Libet's experiment is that the mind cannot be simply what the brain does. For else how could it be that the events in the brain and the events in the mind that are supposedly correlated happen in different orders? If we hear a piano playing the notes G–G–G–Eb but realize that the keys pressed by the pianist are actually G–Eb–G–G we will conclude that it cannot be *this* piano that is producing the sound (assuming that it is a piano that works like all other ones). In a similar way, it is argued, the orchestra of the brain could not play the symphony of consciousness if the presumed sound-causes and the sound-effects are not temporally correlated one-to-one.

This interpretation of Libet's experiments is a minority position and, it strikes me, not the simplest way of accounting for the temporal illusion observed, as it commits us to a nonphysical mind with a considerable degree of causal independence from the brain. The alternative explanation I want to consider does not do this but is in another way just as radical since it has profound consequences for the way in which we see ourselves and our minds.

In order to introduce this explanation it is useful to consider in more detail what is actually supposed to go on when an experience is "referred backward in time." How exactly does the brain play this trick with time? Let us consider an example from the world of magic. Suppose you are a magician planning to perform a spectacular feat of illusion, such as the famous Indian rope trick. There are two different ways in which you can proceed. The first, which I call the *primary* approach, is to give your audience the *experience* of seeing a rope rising into the air. You could do this by a careful arrangement of wires and mirrors on the stage, by some nifty contraption concealed inside the rope, or even by some clever projection that makes your audience think they see a real rope rising, whereas they are in fact only watching a complex computer animation. The precise method is irrelevant; all that matters is that your audience really thinks they see a rope going up into the air.

An alternative method, the *secondary* approach, proceeds in a different way. Here you do not manipulate the audience's experiences but the memories of their experiences. During your performance you might show them some feat that has a certain resemblance to a rope standing up on its own accord, for example, somebody balancing on top of a long, thin bamboo pole.[47] You then subsequently doctor the audience's records of what they have seen into memories of the rope trick. One good way of doing this is to have a long stretch of time pass between the event and the subject's report of the event. In the meantime you will try to restructure their memory by, for example, showing them photographs of the astonishing feat they have supposedly witnessed, or having them talk to other members of the audience who describe matters in exactly the way you want them to be remembered. If, in addition to being a good magician, you are also a skilled neurosurgeon you might attempt to interfere with their memories directly, though given our present-day knowledge of the brain this is perhaps not something to be recommended.

In any case, whether you choose the primary or the secondary approach, the end result is the same. The audience will be in possession of a memory of having seen the rope trick performed, either by being fed manipulated experiences, or by having had their memories tampered with.

Like a skilled magician the brain could use either the primary or the secondary approach to effect backward referral in time. If the primary approach is used then we have to imagine that information processed enters consciousness only after a certain time delay, during which it is possible for the brain to arrange experiences in the desired manner. Remember that the effect of backwards referral in time was supposed to be that we do not experience a skin stimulus five hundred milliseconds after it entered the brain, but more or less simultaneously. So sometime after the five hundred milliseconds the brain would arrange the information such that the experience of the skin sensation appears to happen only ten to twenty milliseconds after the skin was touched, that is, at the time of the primary evoked potential. This doctored version of what really happens is then passed on to consciousness, which will be as convinced that skin stimulus and sensation coincide as a spectator who believes he has just seen the rope trick performed on stage.

---

47. Peter Lamont in his comprehensive study *The Rise of the Indian Rope Trick* (London: Abacus, 2004), pp. 704–8), argues that observations of a pole-balancing feat are what is behind a variety of eyewitness reports of the rope trick.

The secondary approach has the advantage that the time delay required by the primary approach will not be necessary. Here there is no need for buffer time during which potential experiences can be manipulated before they enter consciousness, because first of all we experience what really happens: the five-hundred-millisecond time delay between stimulus and sensation. But immediately afterward this accurate memory is then replaced by an inaccurate one in which the two are seen as coinciding. Irrespective of whether the primary or secondary approach is used, after a few seconds the result will be the same: we believe that stimulus and sensation happened at the same time, even though we have been brought to believe this by different manipulatory routes.

Now it is of course tempting to speculate which of these approaches is actually employed to effect backwards referral in time. But in fact this is an empty question, since both the assumption that the primary approach was chosen and the assumption that the secondary one was chosen account for all the data. According to both accounts the same behavior would result, and subjective experiences of what happens when would be identical as well. The only difference is that with the primary approach an already contaminated experience enters consciousness, whereas with the secondary approach the contamination occurs just after the experience when the memory is changed.

It is now important to realize that we can account for Libet's results and at the same time avoid having to decide the undecidable question of whether backwards referral in time is achieved by the primary or the secondary approach if we *give up the idea that there are always objective facts about the subjective ordering of experiences.* We often find it useful to think of consciousness as a metaphorical theater: this is the place where all the sensory information is displayed after having been processed by the brain. Only what enters the theater is consciously perceived; all other incoming information must remain unconscious. If we think of consciousness as a theater then there is of course an objective order in which experiences enter the theater of consciousness, and there is also a difference between a doctored experience being displayed in the theater, and a manipulated recording of a performance (the memory image of the experience) being shown at a later time.

There are two problems with the metaphor of the theater. First, it postulates a difference between the primary and the secondary approach, even though there is no difference either in the resulting subjective experience or in our behavior. Second, there is also no neurophysiological evidence of such a theater, somewhere "where it all comes together." There is no single place where all the different information entering the brain is integrated; instead, the processing is spread out across the entire brain.

If there is no theater we can simply argue that the problem of temporary ordering of experiences for very small durations is solved by *there being no fact to the matter* as to which experience comes first. The brain can remain flexible about which event precedes which and simply order them in a way that makes the most sense, or causes the least problems for action. There is no need for backwards referral, manipulation of experiences, or manipulation of memories since there is no theater of consciousness where these manipulated displays could be staged. It therefore becomes evident that while, for example, if we think "New York, Paris, Tokyo," we will think "New York" before thinking "Paris," things work in a different manner when we consider very small temporal durations, such as those investigated in the experiments discussed above. In these cases there are no objective facts about which experiences are subjectively earlier than which others.

According to this account, there is no objective fact about which content is "in" consciousness at a given time. A range of pieces of information are processed in the brain simultaneously when we say that some information is conscious, this means that some information is of particular importance for the processing of further content—for example, if it is needed to answer a question, or to interact with the environment in another way. But this can of course vary with the environment we are put in; in one situation one of the many bits of information present in the brain has a particular importance, in another situation another one would. To this extent the content of consciousness cannot be determined without being "probed" in some way—in other words, we cannot determine which piece of content is of particular importance at a given time (and therefore regarded as conscious) without determining how we interact with our surroundings at that time. It is not possible to determine whether a particular experience is conscious by checking where in the brain it is presently being processed.

The upshot of this "theater-less" view of consciousness is that the self disappears as the center of the mind and at best reemerges as a secondary construct. It is not because there is a single self in the theater of consciousness that all our experiences are unified as those of a single experiencer. Rather, the experiences we become conscious of by repeated probing happen to be relatively unified regarding their time, space, and contents so that the pragmatically useful idea of a single observer having all these experiences emerges. It is not the case that the self spins the story of our lives based on conscious contents, but rather that the conscious contents spin us.

We thus realize that one illusion has alerted us to the existence of another, more fundamental one. The temporal illusion of lighting and thunder could be explained by the varying transmission speed of signals. But the similar illusion of the matching of the objective and subjective order of events exemplified by the experiment with stimulation of the brain and the skin could not be dealt with so easily. Here we are led to the conclusion that at the level of small temporal durations there is no right answer to the question of which experience enters consciousness first. And this is best explained by claiming that there is no "entering" of consciousness in the first place. Experiences do not become conscious because they are displayed to the self in an internal theater; rather the experiences themselves create the fictional self unifying them—because there is no theater, there is no show, and no audience either.

WATER BUBBLES

ཆུ་བུར་

WHAT IS ILLUSORY about a water bubble? Very little, we should think. Bubbles are just what they seem to be: small, spherical objects usually found in liquids, such as sparkling or boiling water. Why, then, are they classified as one of the twelve examples of illusion?

It is helpful to look at an occasion when the Buddha himself discussed bubble-related phenomena. One evening he was sitting on the bank of the river Ganges when he saw a great lump of foam floating downstream. What he later said to his monks became known as the *Discourse on Foam* (*Phena sutta*).

> O monks, suppose that this river Ganges was carrying along a great lump of foam. A man with good sight would inspect it, ponder it, and carefully investigate it, and it would appear to him to be void, hollow, insubstantial. So too, o monks, whatever kind of matter there is, whether past, future or present, internal or external, gross or subtle, inferior or superior, far or near, a monk inspects it, ponders it, and carefully investigates it, and it would appear to him to be void, hollow, insubstantial. For what substance could there be in it?

> O monks, suppose that in the autumn, when it is raining and big rain drops are falling, a water bubble rises and bursts on the surface of the water. A man with good sight would inspect it, ponder it, and carefully investigate it, and it would appear to him to be void, hollow, insubstantial. For what substance could there be in a water bubble? So too, o monks, whatever kind of feeling there is, whether past, future or present, internal or external, gross or subtle, inferior or superior, far or near, a monk inspects it, ponders it, and carefully investigates it, and it would appear to him to be void, hollow, insubstantial. For what substance could there be in feeling?

Water bubbles

The Buddha here refers to two different kinds of bubbles: those which make up a lump of foam, and those which rise in agitated water. Foam arises when gas bubbles are trapped in a liquid, resulting in things like frothed milk, sea spray, or the lump of foam on the Ganges the Buddha observed. Foams can create the illusion of looking solid while being anything but; they can fill considerable volume with very little matter. This fact is evident to anyone who ever tried to dry a lump of shaving foam and wondered why there was hardly anything left. It also explains the use of all sorts of synthetic foams as packaging material.

In the passage just cited the Buddha claims that all matter is as insubstantial as foam. In fact this is a very good approximation of how contemporary physics views the constitution of matter. Any object can be decomposed into the molecules that constitute it, which in turn break down into atoms. An atom consists of a tiny nucleus of protons and neutrons circled by a cloud of electrons. The distance between the nucleus and the electrons in relation to their size is astonishing. Trying to locate the nucleus of an atom is indeed, to use the phrase ascribed to the physicist Ernest Rutherford, "like searching for a fly in a cathedral": the electrons surround a tiny bit of matter enclosed in vast amounts of empty space. The neutrons and protons in the nucleus can be decomposed yet further, resulting in a disconcertingly diverse array of subatomic particles. By the 1960s more than a hundred different ones had been discovered. This multifarious zoo was later systematized in what is now known as the standard model, which explains the entire fauna in terms of only twenty-four particles.

String theory, a currently very popular if highly speculative approach, argues that the entire variety of particles found at the subatomic level can be explained in terms of just one fundamental notion: that of a string, a tiny, oscillating, one-dimensional loop about a hundred billion billion (10^{20}) times smaller than an atomic nucleus. Whether there is anything strings are made of is presently an open question. Certainly considering the development of physics over the last century, which revealed more and more subtle layers of matter, it seems unlikely that strings constitute the end of the line. Sooner or later physicists may come up with a theory that explains the behavior of strings by reference to a yet more fundamental entity.

Vasubhandu

Apart from the *physical* questions of what the smallest, indivisible parts of matter (the true "atoms") are, there are also *philosophical* questions concerned with such atoms. These concern the question of whether it is conceptually coherent to assume that the world we live in, which consists of entities with parts, is made up of truly partless things. For the idea that by breaking down things further and further we will eventually arrive at the real atoms of nature, at indivisible, partless things out of which everything is composed, has curious consequences. This has already been observed by the fourth-century Buddhist writer Vasubandhu in a work called *The Twenty Verses*. There he argued that

> if an atom was simultaneously connected with six other atoms it would have six parts. If the six atoms were all in the same place as the atom to which they are connected there would be a single mass the size of an atom.

The problem Vasubandhu has in mind here is the following: Assume there is a conglomerate of seven *real* atoms—indivisible, partless objects. Let us look at a structure consisting of one central atom conglomerated with six other ones. It would look something like this:

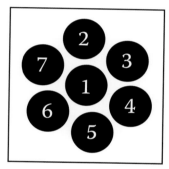

It is evident that atom two and atom five touch atom one at different places. Atom one is between them, so they are not directly touching. But then atom one must have at least two distinct parts: one where it touches atom two and one where it touches atom five, contrary to the assumption that the atoms have no parts.

Alternatively it could be the case that all the seven atoms occupy the same region of space, like this:

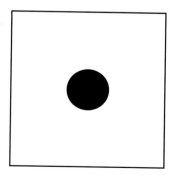

But apart from the difficulty of how distinct objects can ever be at the same time at the same place (this does not hold for ordinary objects: to put your foot in your shoe you have to take the shoe-tree out first), it is now unclear how a conglomeration of atoms can ever fill space. If they all sit together why is *any* macroscopic object bigger than a single atom?

The problem Vasubandhu raises is that for a spread out conglomerate of atoms to occupy space, each of the atoms must have parts (or else they would all coincide), whereas a conglomerate that is not spread out does not manage to cover space. Because of this difficulty, Vasubandhu concludes, the notion of an atom is incoherent.

For Vasubandhu this rejection of atomism is part of a larger philosophical project, since he wants to demonstrate that everything existing is mental in nature. Demonstrating conceptual difficulties with one popular theory for the existence of mind-independent matter, namely atomism, does not yet accomplish that but is nevertheless an important step on the way.

The problem Vasubandhu raises is not easily dissolved, though it may look less problematic if we take into account that some properties of the macroscopic world fail to hold at the microscopic level. It is now well known that the conceptual model of particles as minuscule billiard balls does not get us far in explaining quantum phenomena. A particularly important difference is that while things like billiard balls have both a clearly defined position as well as a speed with which they move, the inability to determine position *and* speed for a single quantum object like a photon at a given moment might lead us to assume that position and momentum are qualities a quantum object cannot have at the same time. What we end up with is a set of probabilities of positions and momenta that indicate the likelihood of different measurements *we would have taken* had we indeed tried to determine their values. But for the setup of Vasubandhu's argument we have to assume that we know both the position and the momentum of all the atoms, something that is impossible for any of the objects contemporary physics considers as candidates for being "true" atoms.

While Vasubandhu's refutation of atomism may thus be guilty of using an inadequate conceptual model to deal with the microworld, using quantum theory as a vindication of atomism seems to be peculiar as well. In fact looking at both the probability distributions quantum theory introduces to explain the behavior of macroscopic objects as well as the crucial role played by the observer, it appears that the Buddha's conception of matter as "foam" was substantial by comparison. The constituents of matter might even be more elusive than the tiny bubbles making up a piece of foam.

Returning to the Buddha's discussion of foam, immediately after his reflections on foam and matter he turns his attention to bubbles, the constituents of foam. Bubbles (soap bubbles, water bubbles, and so forth) are theoretically very interesting entities, because they are a specific kind of hole.[48] A water bubble is a hole in the water, filled with air; a soap bubble is a similarly gas-filled hole in a soapy medium. But what is a hole made of? We might initially want to say that an air-filled hole like a bubble is made of air, perhaps together with a surrounding layer of water. However, it is immediately obvious that we cannot equate holes with the matter that fills them. Consider a bottle. It contains a hole, otherwise we would not be able to fill it with water. But the hole in the bottle cannot consist of the air filling it, since once we fill the bottle with water the air is gone, but the hole is presumably still the same hole. And, to consider an even more extreme case, suppose we put the bottle into a vacuum. Now there is no matter, not even a gas, filling the hole. But the bottle does not suddenly become solid by entering a vacuum, even if there is no filler. So the filler cannot be identified with the hole.

It is easy to overlook the seriousness of the problem posed by holes such as bubbles. A surprisingly large number of people assume that everything that exists in the world is physical. What is generally meant by this is that everything that exists can at least in principle be broken down into its constituting molecules, then into atoms, into subatomic particles, and so forth. Of course there are some things, such as numbers (so-called abstract objects), which are obviously not physical. But these abstract objects have a variety of other properties, such as that the fact that they exist by necessity (what would a world without the number 42 be like?) and that they cannot be causally influenced (try destroying the number 42). But holes are not like numbers. We can easily imagine what it would have meant for a specific hole not to have existed (that bottle could have been made of solid glass) and they can be causally influenced (we can eliminate a hole by putting in a plug). But holes are also not like physical objects. What are the molecules that make up the hole in the glass bottle? They cannot be air molecules, or water molecules, or any other kind.

Now we might want to reply that holes and bubbles can just be regarded as material objects like all other ones. We just have to identify a hole with the inner lining of a hole. So we could say that a water bubble consists of one layer of water molecules surrounding a pocket of air in the water. This is obviously a material object, and we can ask what it is made of. It

---

48. Holes can in turn be subsumed under the category of *absences*, things like a pause in a piece of music, or an interruption in a pattern. Another obvious example of absences are shadows (absences of light), which interestingly often figure in alternative lists of examples of illusion found in the Tibetan literature.

is an arrangement of H_2O molecules in a particular way. But this account faces a variety of problems. First of all it does not agree with many facts we think are true of holes. Take two empty trunks of different sizes and put the smaller insider the bigger one. Now we ordinarily think that the hole enclosed by the smaller trunk is contained in that which is enclosed by the bigger trunk and is part of it. But according to the materialist theory of holes this cannot be the case, since the two holes are just the inner trunk linings, and neither of these is part of the other one. The materialist theory also does not accord with what we can do with holes. Suppose there is a hole with jagged edges in a piece of jelly. If we scoop out some more jelly, thereby smoothing out the edges, we have enlarged the hole. But we have not enlarged the hole lining. In fact we may have reduced it, since the surface of the hole with the jagged edges would have been greater than the surface of the smooth-edged hole.

But if bubbles and holes are not material objects, then what are they? They are mere absences, places where some surrounding medium, such as water, or a soap solution, is not. Even though they deceptively look like familiar objects such as marbles, baubles, or crystal balls, unlike these things bubbles and holes are not material objects. There is nothing a bubble is made of. Whereas everyday objects like marbles and baubles depend for their existence on their parts—the small bits of glass or crystal constituting them—holes such as bubbles completely depend on the constitution of other things, such as the surrounding water. The water molecules have to be arranged in a particular way for there to be a bubble, and this is all the bubble can possibly depend on for its existence. Despite looking like ordinary objects, they are not. There are no bubble-atoms.

In the passage from the *Discourse on Foam* cited at the beginning of this chapter the Buddha uses the example of bubbles to illustrate the nature of feeling, one of the five components of a person mentioned in traditional Buddhist philosophy.

It might be intuitively plausible to hold something like an "atomic" theory of feelings. Feelings could be seen as coming in different kinds (pleasurable, painful, and neutral), and in different sizes (intensities) within these kinds. On this account an important goal in life appears to be to maximize the occurrence of pleasurable feelings and minimize the occurrence of painful and neutral ones. Our pursuit of happiness seems therefore to entail the striving for an ideally unbroken succession of pleasurable feelings of as high an intensity as we can achieve.

In fact this intuitive idea was developed in considerable detail by the English philosopher Jeremy Bentham in his "Hedonistic Calculus" (sometimes

The mummified body of Jeremey Bentham in its display cabinet

also called "Utilitarian Calculus"). Bentham develops a set of parameters for gauging the value of a feeling. These include its *intensity*, its *duration*, the *certainty* of its occurrence, its *propinquity* (how far in the future it is located), and its *fecundity* (how likely it is that this pleasure will lead to further pleasures). Bentham developed his system with a considerable degree of sophistication, in particular since his account not only incorporated individual pleasures and pains, but also those of other people.

There are, however, two fundamental problems with the underlying "atomic" theory of feelings. To understand the first difficulty it is necessary to get an idea of the notion of an *expectation horizon*. This describes our expectation of what is going to happen in the future. Events situated qualitatively above the expectation horizon are experienced as pleasure, those below it as pain. We can also correlate the distance from the horizon with the intensity of the feeling: the greater the distance, the more intense the feeling. To illustrate this point with a simple example, suppose you are waiting for a train and, based on your past experiences, expect it to be up to five minutes delayed. If it is only two minutes delayed this event will be located above your expectation horizon and will be experienced as pleasure. If, however, it is ten minutes late this will be below your horizon and will therefore be regarded as painful or unpleasant. The interesting (and problematic) fact now is that the expectation horizon tends to move with the quality of what we experience. The more pleasure we experience the more the horizon moves up, the more unpleasant our life is, the more it moves down. This might be due to the fact that we use some sort of similarity forecasting when projecting our expectation horizon into the future: we expect things to turn out in the future more or less the same as they are now or were in the not-too-distant past. A succession of events above our horizon will then turn into a new status quo, and events that we experience as similarly pleasurable will have to have the same relative distance to the new horizon as the old horizon had to the previous events. The difficulty inherent in this picture is now apparent. If things are going well, our expectation horizon goes up. In order to derive the same relative satisfaction in the future, things must go even better. If they do, our horizon goes up still farther, and so on. Psychologists have labeled this phenomenon the "hedonic treadmill" because like a man on a treadmill who has to keep moving just to stay in the same place, we have to achieve more and more pleasure just to derive the same level of satisfaction.

The comparison of feelings with atoms is therefore misleading: an atom has its weight no matter which device we use for measuring it, but the intensity of a pleasurable feeling does not just depend on *it*, it depends on where our baseline is located. But if this is right it has profound consequences for the way we should act. Following the hedonic calculus now seems like a very bad idea. Suppose we do this and strive after as many intensely pleasurable sensations as we can. If we are successful we invariably raise our horizon. But assuming that many or most events that befall us are beyond our control, raising the horizon will increase the number of events that fall below the horizon and are therefore experienced as unpleasant or downright painful. If we have a machine shooting tennis balls at a net at more or less random angles, the more we raise the net the smaller the number going over it will be. It turns out that pursuing the hedonic calculus is the best recipe for making us less happy rather than more so.

The second difficulty with an atomistic theory of feelings is that it makes sense to conceptualize pleasure and pain not as two distinct kinds of things but rather to regard one as an absence of the other. In the same way as there are not two kinds of stuff, water-stuff and bubble-stuff, but only water-stuff, the *absence* of which constitutes a bubble, pleasure can be seen as the absence of pain (or, the other way around, pain as the absence of pleasure). In the first case pleasure would not be a basic psychological element but merely the absence of pain.

An interesting experiment in support of this idea has recently been carried out on fruit flies. The fruit flies were divided into two groups. The first was exposed to an odor, followed by a painful electric shock. After little time the flies learned to avoid the odor, assuming it to be a warning sign for the shock to follow. The second group was also given an electric shock but was exposed to the odor *afterward*. Interestingly enough, the flies in the second group, far from avoiding the odor, actually moved toward it. In the same way the first group regarded the odor as the indicator of something painful, the second group regarded it as an indicator of something pleasant, hence they actively sought it. But the only pleasurable thing connected with the odor was the absence of pain after the electric shock. So it appears that in this example something could be regarded as pleasurable not because it is accompanied by any intrinsically pleasurable sensation but merely by being accompanied by the absence of a painful one.

That pleasure is nothing but the absence of pain was also argued by the Tibetan philosopher Tsong kha pa (1357–1419). In his monumental survey of Buddhism, called *The Great Exposition of the Stages of the Path*, he writes:

> Moreover, your current pleasant feelings—which cause attachment to grow—mostly arise only upon the relief of suffering; pleasure does not exist naturally, independently of the removal of suffering. For example, if you suffer because of too much walking, a pleasant state of mind arises when you sit down. Then, as the earlier intense suffering fades, pleasure appears to arise gradually. Yet sitting is not naturally pleasant, because if you sit too long, suffering arises again, just as before.

Thus we should not think that the pleasant feeling we have sitting down after walking all day is an accumulation of pleasure-atoms; rather it is a result of the gradual lessening of pain. But it would be just as hasty to conclude that therefore pleasures are simply the absence of pain-atoms as it was to conclude that bubbles are the absence of water molecules. What we have to realize is that the situation is completely symmetric. Suppose I promise to take you out for a fancy meal in the evening and then tell you just before that I did not manage to get a table. Having a normal dinner instead you might now be annoyed, even though objectively nothing has changed. You take less pleasure in your dinner because of comparing it to the delicious one you could have had. In other words the pain you experience is not due to the fact that your dinner is intrinsically unpleasant; the pain is merely due to the absence of pleasure that might have been.

But now we have to ask ourselves which position is the right one: are pains or pleasures the basic building blocks of our emotional life? That there seem to be equally good arguments either way might point to a difficulty with an underlying assumption, namely that there are any atomic feelings at all. Pain and pleasure are interdependent. Pleasure would not be very pleasurable if there was no pain to serve as a contrast, nor would pain presumably be experienced as pain in the absence of pleasure. We cannot have one without the other, as we cannot have water bubbles without having water. Pleasure and pain are not substantial components out of which our emotional life is built. Rather they are interconnected entities, like the bubble and the water: if one increases the other is reduced, and vice versa. Attempting to eliminate one in favor of the other a hopeless enterprise.

We thus see that the Buddha's similes of the foam and the bubble expose two illusions that come up all the time in our everyday interaction with the world. We think that matter is solid, even though it is anything but—in fact considering the elusive nature of its fundamental constituents even foam seems substantial by comparison. We also think that feelings are solid: that what gives us a pleasant feeling now will continue to do so in the future, that to evade pain and suffering we just have to increase the amount of pleasurable sensations, thereby outnumbering if not completely obliterating the unpleasant ones. But if we consider the nature of pleasure and pain we realize that this feat cannot be done: not just because we are too feeble or incompetent, but as a matter of necessity. Seeing through this latter illusion is very likely to change the way in which we lead our lives.

A REFLECTION
IN A MIRROR

ཨེ་ལོང་ནང་གི་གཟུགས་བརྙན་

WHEN A TIBETAN painted scroll or *thangka*[49] showing one of the many deities of the Buddhist pantheon has been finished by the artist, it is not yet complete. It is still only a collection of paint on a piece of canvas, not yet a holy object. To become an object of worship it has to be consecrated. Such a consecration is a complex ritual during which holy texts are recited, flowers are thrown, and incense is burned. The aim is to invite the deity depicted to reside in the painting itself so that the image can fulfill its religious purpose. Once the deity has done so, various offerings are made to it, including the offering of a bath. To this end the painting is reflected in a mirror, which is then immersed in water, or at least sprinkled with it. Only after this is done can the painting really be regarded as blessed by the deity's presence.

In a slightly different context the same ritual is described as follows.

Thus with a crash of peaceful music they visualize that they have invited all the Buddhas and Bodhisattvas, and to them—in the person of the image on the altar—they proceed to offer a welcoming bath. The altar server reflects the image in a small mirror, and it is upon the reflection of the image that he begins to pour water from the washing flask as the assembly sings: . . .

Just as the Buddha, as soon as he was born,
was bathed by all the gods,
I pray you likewise bathe your body
with this pure divine water.

---

49. བྱང་ག་

Two Tibetan painters
at work

The idea of bathing something by bathing its mirror image might strike us as slightly peculiar, like attempting to shave the image we see in the bathroom mirror, rather than shaving ourselves. On the one hand the use of a mirror in this ritual of "offering the bath" is of a purely practical nature. The colors a Tibetan artist uses to paint a religious scroll consist of pigments bound by water-soluble hide glue. Sprinkling such a painting with water is not a good idea, as it would permanently disfigure it. However, these pragmatic concerns are only one part of the explanation, and perhaps not even the most important one. This is evident from the fact that the same consecration rituals are used for images not easily damaged by contact with water, such as statues.

The second part of the explanation of the ritual is that both the image and its reflection in the mirror are regarded as having the same degree of reality. The reflection in the mirror, the deity itself, and the image it resides in are regarded as having the same existential status. For this reason bathing the one is as good as bathing the other, since there is no fundamental difference between the two.

A Tibetan mirror

In the Tibetan literature we find a variety of spiritual exercises based on ascribing the same degree of reality to a thing and its reflection in a mirror. A short text called *A Primer on the Six Yogas of Nāropa*[50] describes a meditation aimed at establishing emotional equanimity as follows:

> Standing before a mirror, observe the reflection of your own body— looking at the image for some time—and consider how this image is produced by a combination of various factors—the mirror, body, light, space, etc.—under certain conditions. It is an object of dependent-arising without any substance, appearing, yet void.
>
> Then observe the appearance of the image together with its clothes and ornaments, and consider whether you are pleased or displeased with it; again feign to burst into anger, fight against yourself, and observe whether you are affected by it. Practicing thus, you will discover that all pleasures and displeasures are illusory, created by one's own mind, and your grasping at them will be greatly reduced.

The equanimity developed toward the person seen behind the mirror can of course only be transferred toward other people around us, which exist in front of the mirror, if both types of persons are regarded as having the same degree of reality or, as the Tibetan writers would prefer to put it, if both are seen as lacking substantial reality to the same extent.

In a different set of practices the practitioner visualizes his tutelary divinity[51] in front of him. Again our text recommends the use of mirrors:

> Procure a very clear painting of the tutelary divinity, place it between two mirrors and observe the illusoriness of the three images. Use the picture as an aid to visualize the tutelary divinity, until it appears as clear in your mind as the beloved in that of a lover. One should visualize the complete image of the whole body all at once, and hold it clearly as long as possible. After a while the vision will fade and one should then visualize a given part of the divinity's body until it becomes extremely clear. One should start with the head and face; then the neck, upper body, limbs, and so forth; until the whole body becomes extremely clear.

---

50. ནུ་རོ་ཆོས་དྲུག་གི་ཀ་དཔེ་
51.ཡི་དམ་

At a later stage the meditator will then identify his own body with that of the tutelary divinity visualized with the aid of the mirror image, thereby seeing himself as the deity. Once again the apparently solid boundary between objects on the different sides of the mirror is dissolved.

We might think that the assumption underlying all these practices, that of ascribing the same status to an object and its reflection, is somewhat bizarre. After all, ordinary objects are things we can access with all our five senses, while mirror images can only be seen. We cannot really interact with them in the way we can with objects in front of the mirror. On the whole reflections in a mirror appear to be considerably less real than the objects they reflect.

In order to understand what the Buddhist writers could have meant by regarding ordinary objects as similar to mirror images we have to get a better idea of what mirror images really are. It is surprising that very few people have a clear understanding of how these come about and why they have the properties they do. Despite the fact that we are constantly surrounded by mirrors and are very familiar with our own mirror image, it is easy to be confused about its nature. Often people think that what they see in a mirror is just what somebody standing where the mirror is would see. The idea is that if your mirror was no mirror fixed to the wall but a transparent piece of glass covering a window, the image you see while shaving is what somebody looking in through the window would see. But this is not true. Seeing yourself in a mirror is not seeing yourself as others would see you, or as you would see yourself on a photograph. What the mirror shows is your *enantiomorph*.

Imagine the spiral on the left (opposite page) was printed on a piece of transparent plastic. No matter how you turned and moved it across the page, you could never make it coincide with the spiral on the right, which is its mirror image. It is this fact that makes one spiral an enantiomorph of another. The only way in which you could make them coincide is by lifting the piece of plastic up, turning it around, and putting it back on the page. If the above figure had been a circle, however, none of this would have been necessary. Just by moving a circle you can make it coincide with its mirror image. For this reason circles and similar figures are called nonchiral. A spiral is chiral, or "handed," because its mirror image is an enantiomorph. You cannot make a left-turning spiral coincide with its right-turning mirror image.

The human body is chiral too. Even though its left and right half look quite symmetrical, since there is a left leg corresponding to the right leg, a left ear corresponding to the right ear, etc., in fact they are not. This is quite

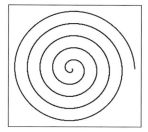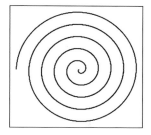

Left, a spiral; right, its enantiomorph

apparent when we "compose" a human face by joining one half of it with its enantionmorph.

Now imagine you stand three steps away from a full-length mirror. Assume the mirror is taken out and there is a hole in the wall behind it. You walk three steps, go through the hole, make another three steps, and spin around on your heel. You are now standing where your mirror image used to be. Supposing your mirror image was still there, would the two of you coincide? The answer is no, because of the chirality of the human body. You and your mirror image would have your hearts on opposite sides of your bodies. If you are right-handed, the mirror image is left-handed. If you are missing an arm, the mirror image will have an arm in this place but lack one on the other side.

But once we have seen through the illusion that our mirror image is something other people would see if they stood where the mirror stands, and recognize that it is something one could *only* see in a mirror and nowhere else, a different puzzling issue arises.

Left, a real face; right, a composite face

A mirror is a two-dimensional thing: it has horizontal width (left and right) and vertical height (up and down). Now my mirror image has left and right reversed everywhere: his wristwatch is on the other arm, his shirt buttons right over left, and so forth. But he still has his feet on the ground and his head up in this air. This is very peculiar. For after all if mirrors do reverse, why do they not reverse everything, that is, why do they not reverse both dimensions, left and right *and* up and down? The mirror is not going to know the difference between the dimensions. Moreover, the reversal is not affected even if I turn the mirror around or put it on the floor. Real "up" is mirror "up" and real "down" is mirror "down," but real "right" is mirror "left" and real "left" is mirror "right."

Now let us do a little mental acrobatics. Suppose you want to join your mirror image at the other side of the mirror. What do you do? Here is the easy way: go up to the mirror, which, just as Alice experienced in *Through the Looking-Glass*, will melt away "just like a bright silvery mist," pass right through it, and turn around. You are now standing next to your mirror image. Next consider a somewhat more daring way: step back a bit, run toward the mirror, jump, pass through it with a forward somersault in such a way that you come to rest upside-down with your head on that of your mirror image. (Fortunately you only have to do this in your imagination.)

As you try to keep your balance, reflect on what has happened: now your mirror image is reversed top-to-bottom relative to you, but not left to right. Your hearts are on the same side, but his feet are where his head should be. What has happened?

In order to understand the results of this acrobatic act, consider how mirrors work. A ray of light coming from some object will hit the mirror and is reflected back at the same angle. If this reflected angle now hits your retina you see something in the mirror. In the first diagram on page 168, the observer (located where the eye is) sees the reflection of the inscription of two letters, *T* and *M*, which are located to his left, reflected in the mirror. The light ray coming from the *T* is represented by a dotted line, that coming from the *M* by a straight line.

Up to this point matters are very simple. The interesting fact now is that we implicitly assume that rays of light travel in straight lines. For this reason we do not see the light bouncing off the inscription as coming from the left of us (which it really is) but as coming straight toward us *from behind the mirror*. This is why the mind constructs the mirror space, namely the space we think we would see if the mirror was a window. Of course we all know

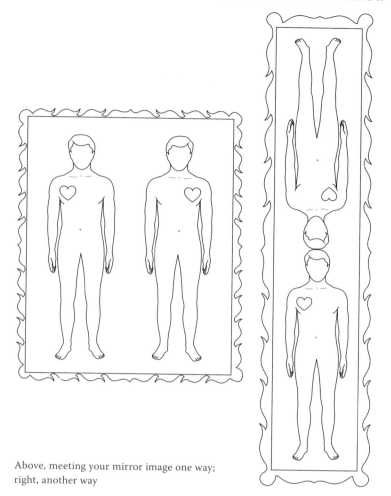

Above, meeting your mirror image one way;
right, another way

that a mirror is no window, and that there is no space behind it, but this is yet another example of an illusion that will not go away even if we know it is one.

What is happening, therefore, is that the source of the light rays that is to our left is considered to be in front of us, that is, it is projected into mirror space. In the diagram this is done by mentally flipping the bundle of light rays coming toward the eye sideways, along the direction of the arrow. After this flip the source of the image is experienced as something in front of us.

Now it is interesting to note that this "flip" could also be done in a different way, namely upward and then down. This is shown in the bottom diagram on the next page. In this case we do not "slide" the bundle of light rays sideways parallel to the ground and into the mirror space, as in the

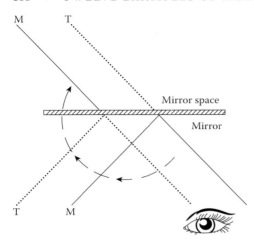

Projection into mirror-space

previous diagram, but we "lift it up" parallel to a vertical axis and then fold it down into mirror space. The resulting image is then reversed top to bottom, and not left to right.

Now one might think that there is something wrong with this alternative projection. For we know that when we look at the letters *T M* in a mirror we see *M T*, as shown in the first diagram, and not an upside-down *T* followed by an upside-down *M*. Therefore we can just check by simple inspection that the left-right dimension is reversed, and *not* the up-down dimension.

The problem with this objection is that it already presupposes that we project ourselves into the mirror by a sideways motion, rather than by an upward flip. Assume your projection into the mirror space was balancing on its head on the top of the sequence *T M*. What you would see from this perspective is an upside-down letter *T* on the left, with an upside-down letter *M* to its left, exactly as shown in the second diagram.

This implies that you cannot decide questions about the orientation of things in the mirror space just by looking at how things appear to you. Such

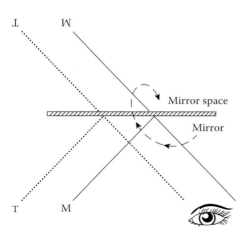

An alternative projection into mirror-space

an appearance necessarily relies on an assumption about your own orientation in the mirror space. But how you project yourself into the mirror is determined neither by the laws of the world in front of the mirror, nor by anything going on behind it. As far as it is up to us how we project ourselves into the mirror space, it is up to us what mirrors invert, the horizontal or the vertical dimension. It merely appears to us that mirrors invert the horizontal rather than the vertical dimension because we have an automatic way of thinking of ourselves in mirror space and rarely consider alternatives that are equally possible.

Why we have such an automatic preference for one way of projection is an interesting question. One possible answer is that this depends on the comparative ease with which we can move images recalled from memory in the different directions of mental space. To experience what we see in the mirror as left-and-right reversed we have to revert our recalled image of the object along the horizontal dimension (we have to see it backward, so to speak). But for the alternative view depicted in the second diagram we have to reverse the image up-and-down. There is some evidence that such reversal involves more cognitive resources than left-and-right reversal. We rarely have to identify something standing on its head in daily life, so the brain lacks a specific mechanism for dealing with this problem. For example, we find it very easy to identify left-and-right inverted faces, but recognizing people in upside-down photographs is surprisingly difficult. Our "normal" way of projecting images into the mirror space is therefore the one generally chosen because it uses the least cognitive resources.

But apart from such psychological facts, there is no fundamental difficulty in assuming a world in which the kind of inversion shown in the second diagram was the one we usually made. We can easily imagine a set of people who have a concept of horizontal directions that is not inverted by a mirror. Assume that instead of the terms "left" and "right" they used the terms "cordial" and "discordial," where the cordial side of your body is the one where your heart is. If you hold a book in your left hand your mirror image will hold it in his right hand. But if you hold it in your cordial hand, so will your mirror image.

Now assume this tribe also had a set of terms for the two ends of the body, the "noble end" and the "base end," defined in an analogous manner as our terms for left and right. We define "left" as what is west of you if your head is up and you are facing north. Similarly, the noble end of your body is what is up when your cordial side is west and you are facing north. Now a mirror *will* invert the noble and the base ends of your body: if you are wearing shoes on your base end your mirror image will be wearing them on its noble end. Once again, which dimensions the mirror is seen to invert will depend on which concepts of dimensions we happen to employ.

We are suffering from an illusion if we think we could just determine the properties of a mirror image by looking. As the preceding discussion showed, reflections in a mirror are a particularly clear example of the fact that there is no "innocent eye," that looking at the world will not let us see anything unless we come equipped with a substantial set of assumptions about what we think we will see, assumptions that are generally not evident to us. The question of whether a mirror image would appear inverted along the horizontal or vertical dimension for an objective observer therefore makes no sense. The image we see in the mirror is the image we have constructed, depending on the way we project ourselves into mirror space. Independent of such a projection there is simply no image there for us to see.

Another issue we have to address when considering the Buddhist claim that mirror images and ordinary objects have a similar existential status are the *effects* mirror images have. One reason why mirror images appear less real to us than the world they reflect is because the causal exchange between the worlds on the two sides of the mirror is not equal. Our world is the cause of all the objects in mirror space, but the objects there cause very little in the real world, apart from cut-free shaves and well-adjusted ties.

However, there is an interesting case that shows us that this view of mirror images as little more than epiphenomena, as something that is caused but does not cause back, is not always useful. This case is the treatment of patients with a phantom limb.

More than half of patients who have lost a limb suffer from the irritating illusion that it is somehow still there. This illusion can be surprisingly strong, to the extent that the patient still feels the results of using his phantom limb. The neuroscientist Vilayanur Ramachandran, one of the best known researchers into phantom limbs, tells the story of his patient whom he asked to lift a cup with his phantom hand. Just as he is about the reach out with the stump of his arm Ramachandran pulls the cup away. The patient cries out in pain. What is the explanation? The patient was just reaching through the cup handle and has felt the pain of his illusory fingers being twisted as the cup was pulled away. Even though the twisted finger was illusory, the pain experienced by the patient was as real as the cup that caused it.

Phantom limbs can be extremely distressing for the patient, for they are often experienced as painful, burning, itching, or twisted into uncomfortable positions. In addition they are not easy to treat, not least because there is nothing to be found where the patient says the pain is coming from. In the past it was generally thought that the pain experienced in phantom limbs was the result of an inflammation of the nerve endings where the limb had been amputated. The nonsensical information that these nerves ending nowhere would then send back to the brain was experienced as pain. As a treatment sometimes a second amputation was carried out in order to remove the stump with the affected nerve endings, thereby stopping the pain at least temporarily. This tended not to be very successful; sometimes patients were not just left with the pain of the phantom limb but also experienced additional pain in the phantom stump.

Ramachandran developed a novel treatment for phantom limbs based on the assumption that the source of the trouble was not due to inflamed nerve endings, but had more complex cognitive causes. He argued that what happens in the case of phantom limbs stuck in painfully twisted positions is that whenever the brain tried to move the limb there was no feedback returning to the brain. After a while the brain learned that the limb was paralyzed (rather than that there was no limb there anymore). This fiction of the brain, the illusory paralyzed limb, was the cause of the pain the patient experienced.

Based on this idea, Ramachandran came up with a new course of treatment. If the brain could somehow be convinced that the missing limb could still be moved, it might unlearn its assumption that the limb is paralyzed and stuck in an uncomfortable position, thereby removing the pain. But how does one move an object that does not exist? To do this Ramachandran constructed a device called the *mirror box*.

This is a simple wooden box with two holes and a mirror serving as a middle partition. In the case of a patient with a left phantom hand he would put his right hand through the right hole and the stump through the left hole. The top of the left half of the box would then be covered. As the patient looks into the right half he seems to see his left hand restored—it is the left-and-right reversed mirror image of his right hand. If the patient now makes a fist with his right hand it looks as if his left is clenching in unison. It appears to the brain as if it is indeed able to move the paralyzed phantom hand together with the healthy right hand.

Somewhat surprisingly, this very simple treatment of a very complex condition has led to the long-term improvement of many patients suffering from phantom limbs stuck in painful positions. Ramachandran's mirror box provides us with an interesting example of a case where a mirror image actually has a causal effect on the real world. We usually think of mirror images as mere reflections of the world in front of the mirror with no causal influence on it whatsoever. We cannot light a cigarette with a flame seen in a mirror. That the mirror image is not just a passive reflection but a relatively com-

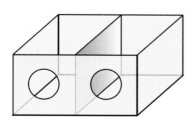

Mirror box

plex active construction on our part became evident in the discussion of left-and-right reversal. It is now clear that mirror images can also sometimes influence the real world in unexpected ways. The moving hand is illusory, because there is no real hand moving where we see it (we only think there is) but its effect is *not* illusory. We do not just *think* that the pain in the phantom limb is removed, but it really is removed.

When Buddhist philosophers speak of the things around us as illusory like a reflection in mirror there are two important points this comparison tries to convey. First of all, even though things appear to be, like a mirror image, right there in front of us, they are not just "out there" no matter what, waiting to be let into our minds by the doors of perception. What we find in the world is the result of a complex process of cognitive construction, an artifact shaped by our minds in ways we are often not aware of. As became evident in the discussion of left-right reversal, what we see is heavily dependent on assumptions we make, and if we made very different assumptions, we would see a very different world. Knowing about these assumptions usually does not make much of a difference to how things appear to us. No matter how often we convince ourselves that there is no space behind the mirror, and that the only existence the mirror-space could possibly have is in our minds, whenever we look into the mirror the mirror-space and all the objects in it are laid out in front of us, evident to everybody and appearing very much like ordinary space.

Secondly, the fact that the things around us are mind-dependent cognitive constructs does not keep them from being able to act as causes that bring about results. The illusory left hand can alleviate the pain of the phantom limb, and it seems that *only* an illusory hand could have done so. Using a real hand, for example attached to another body, would not have worked, because this real hand could not be moved by the patient, while he could move the illusory hand. Nor would a completely "illusion-free" approach, for example by instructing the patient to tell his brain that it is wrong in assuming there is a paralyzed limb attached to his body, have been very effective. That things depend for their existence on our minds, like the mirror-image of the right hand, does not preclude them from appearing as standing in relations of cause and effect.

We might interpret the mirror box experiment as a case of an illusory cause (the mirrored hand) having a real effect (the removal of the pain). This would not let it come out as a very good example of the Buddhist view of things, since in that case both cause and effect would be regarded as similarly illusory. But then we might equally argue that we only call the pain "real" because it tends to be more stable than other things. If the patient with the mirror tries to grasp something with his "two" hands we quickly realize that the left hand has not really been restored to him. But the pain in the phantom limb tends to hang around and is hardly influenced by what we do with the limb. So we might argue that even in this example both cause and effect can be regarded as illusory. What we call real are not things "being there anyway," but simply the more persistent illusions.

REFERENCES AND
FURTHER READING

The story about the Indian king can be found in Candrakīrti's commentary on verse 72 of Āryadeva's *Catuḥśataka*. For an English summary see Ruth Sonam: *Yogic Deeds of Bodhisattvas* (Ithaca, N.Y.: Snow Lion, 1994), page 112.

INTRODUCTION

The text of the མདོ་རྒྱུད་བསྟན་བཅོས་དུ་མ་ནས་འབྱུང་བའི་ཚོམས་ཀྱི་རྣམ་གྲངས་ཤེས་ལྡན་ཡིད་ཀྱི་དགའ་སྟོན་ཞེས་བྱ་བ་ can be found on folios 465–531 in volume 7 of *The Collected Works of* དཀོན་མཆོག་འཇིགས་མེད་ དབང་པོ, *the Second* འཇམ་དབྱངས་བཞད་པ *of* ལ་བྲང་བཀྲ་ཤིས་འཁྱིལ, 12 volumes (New Delhi: Demo, 1971).

An introduction to Prajñāpāramitā texts can be found in Edward Conze's *The Prajñāpāramitā Literature* ('s Gravenhage Mouton, 1960). The iconography of the personification of Prajñāpāramitā is discussed on pages. 14–16. Conze has translated a number of Prajñāpāramitā texts, including the version of the recensions in 25,000 and 100,000 lines as *The Large Sutra on Perfect Wisdom, with the Divisions of the Abhisamayālaṃkāra* (Berkeley: University of California Press, 1975). His *Short Prajñāpāramitā Texts* (London: Luzac & Co., 1973) contains a useful collection of the shorter recensions, including the *Perfection of Wisdom in One Letter* on page 242.

A brief but very clear discussion of the contents of the most famous of Prajñāpāramitā texts, the *Heart Sutra*, is in chapter 16 of Peter Della Santina's *The Tree of Enlightenment* (Taiwan: Chico Dharma Study Foundation, 1997), pages 141–48. For a more detailed treatment see Donald Lopez's *The Heart Sūtra Explained: Indian and Tibetan Commentaries* (Albany: State University of New York Press, 1988).

The quotation from Thomas Metzinger comes from his book *The Ego Tunnel: The Science of the Mind and the Myth of the Self* (New York: Basic Books, 2009), page. On the connection between intellectual insight and the continued appearance of an illusion, see page 111.

MAGIC སྒྱུ་མ

The account of the miracles in Śrāvastī is taken from Buddhaghosa's *Dhamma-padaṭṭhakathā*, translated by Eugene Burlingame in his *Buddhist Legends* (Cambridge, Mass.: Harvard University Press, 1921), part 3, pages 41–47. A description of the Ajatashatru pillar is given in Ananda Coomaraswamy's *La sculpture de Bharhut* (Paris: Vanoest, 1956), pages 53–54.

The description of the later performance of the mango trick is to be found in Vendla von Langenn's *Bettler, Heilige und Maharajas: Indienreise einer Frau* (Stuttgart: Deutsche Verlags-Anstalt, 1949), pages 152–53, which describes her travels in India in the 1930s. The books contains numerous photographs that are considerably more inspiring than the prose.

Various descriptions of the mango trick from historical accounts of the sixteenth and seventeenth centuries can be found in Henry Yule and A.C. Burnell's *Hobson-Jobson: A Glossary of Colloquial Anglo-Indian Words and Phrases, and of Kindred Terms, Etymological, Historical, Geographical and Discursive*, new edition, edited by William Crooke (London: Murray, 1903), s.v. "mango trick," pages 555–56.

It is interesting to note that the mango trick is also described in Chinese texts where it is attributed to Taoist magicians and performed not with mangoes, but with a variety of indigenous flora, such as melons, pears, and peonies—a delightful version involving pears can be found in the 聊齋誌異 by Pu Songling (蒲松齡), translated into English by John Minford as *Strange Tales from a Chinese Studio* (London: Penguin, 2006), pages 47–49. For a long and somewhat rambling article on this topic see Robert van Gulik's "The 'Mango Trick' in China," *Transactions of the Asiatic Society of Japan*, 3rd ser., 3 (1954), pages 117–69.

For the description of the illusory double in the *Sāmaññaphalasutta* see Maurice Walshe's translation, *Thus Have I Heard: The Long Discourses of the Buddha (Dīgha Nikāya)* (London: Wisdom, 1987), pages 104–5. The *Mahāsakuludāyisutta* can be found in *The Middle Length Discourses of the Buddha*, translated by Bhikkhu Ñāṇamoli and Bhikkhu Bodhi (Boston Wisdom, in association with the Barre Center for Buddhist Studies, 1995).

Gyal tshab je's བཞི་བརྒྱ་པའི་རྣམ་བཤད་ལེགས་བཤད་སྙིང་པོ can be found in volume ཀ of his *Collected Works* (གསུལ་ཆེན་རྟེའི་གསུང་འབུམ, Dharamsala: Shes rigs par khang, 1981). There is an English translation by Ruth Sonam called *Yogic Deeds of Bodhisattvas* (Ithaca, N.Y.: Snow Lion, 1994). The passage cited can be found on page 287.

An account of the various magical phenomena Alexandra David-Néel claims to have witnessed in Tibet can be found in chapter 8 of her *Mystiques et magiciens du Thibet* (Paris: Plon, 1929). The translation is from the first English edition (London: Lave, 1931).

An English translation of the *Visuddhimagga* by Bhikkhu Ñāṇamoli was published in 1975 as *The Path of Purification* by the Buddhist Publication Society in Kandy, Sri Lanka; it was published by Shambhala in Berkeley, California, in 1976. The passage quoted is on page 444. The quotations from W. Y. Evans-Wentz come from footnote 1 on page 29 of his *Tibetan Book of the Great Liberation* (Oxford: Oxford University Press, 1954).

Some information on the illusion of neon color spreading can be found in H.F.J.M. van Tuijl's "A New Visual Illusion: Neonlike Color Spreading and Complementary Color Induction between Subjective Contours," *Acta Psychologica* 39 (1975), pages 441–45; the illusion of the continuous sound is described in R. M. Warren's "Perceptual Restoration of Obliterated Sounds," *Psychological Bulletin* 96, no. 2 (1984), pages 371–83.

A description of an interesting case of visual anosognosia can be found in Oliver Sacks's *An Anthropologist on Mars* (New York: Knopf, 1995), in a chapter called "The Last Hippie."

The time-gap experience is discussed on pages 18–20 of Graham Reed's *The Psychology of Anomalous Experience* (London: Hutchinson, 1972).

The final quotation from the Buddha comes from the *Khandasaṃyutta*. For the context of this statement see volume 1 of Bhikkhu Bodhi's *The Connected Discourses of the Buddha: A New Translation of the Saṃyutta Nikāya* (Boston: Pali Text Society and Wisdom Publications, 2001), pages 951–53.

THE MOON IN THE WATER 水月

A French translation of the *Mahāprajñāpāramitāśāstra* attributed to Nāgārjuna can be found in Étienne Lamotte's *Le traité de la grande vertu de sagesse* (Louvain: Bureaux du Muséon, 1944). The passage quoted is on page 364.

The non-existence of the self is also argued for in some contemporary theories of cognitive science. See, e.g., Thomas Metzinger, *The Ego Tunnel: The Science of the Mind and the Myth of the Self* (New York: Basic Books, 2009), page 208. For the evolutionary uses of the notion of a self see pages 64–65.

An early discussion of the nature of the face seen in the moon can already be found in Plutarch's *De facie in orbe lunae*. For an English translation see pages 1–223 of volume 12 of the Loeb Classical Library edition of his *Moralia,* translated by Harold Cherniss and W.C. Helmbold (London: Heinemann, 1957).

More Tibetan depictions of the rabbit in the moon as well as some iconographic background can be found on plate 65 and pages 120–21 of Robert Beer's *Encyclopedia of Tibetan Symbols and Motifs* (Boston: Shambhala, 1999). This also gives a drawing of the red three-legged bird that is sometimes depicted in the sun. Plate 20 presents examples of rocks shown in Tibetan paintings that were made to look like various Buddhist ritual implements. For more on the background of similar hidden images, including the Chinese *i p'in* (異品) style of painting, see H.W. Janson's entry on "chance images" in the *Dictionary of the History of Ideas* (New York: Scribner, 1973–1974), volume 1, pages 340–53.

In his *Demon-Haunted World: Science as a Candle in the Dark* (New York: Ballantine, 1997), Carl Sagan notes further images projected onto the moon:

> In world myth and folklore, many images are seen: a woman weaving, strands of laurel trees, an elephant jumping off a cliff, a girl with a basket on her back, a rabbit, the lunar intestines spilled out on its surface after evisceration by an irritable flightless bird, a woman pounding tapa cloth, a four-eyed jaguar. People of one culture have trouble understanding how such bizarre things could be seen by the people of another.

The quotation from Galileo's *Sidereus Nuncius* comes from the translation in Stillman Drake's *Discoveries and Opinions of Galileo* (Garden City, N.Y.: Doubleday, 1957), page 36. For a study of Galileo's observations of the moon with extensive references, the reader is referred to part 9 of Paul Feyerabend's *Against Method*, 3rd ed. (London: Verso,

1993). For a more recent (and more popular) account readers might want to consult chapter 11 of Roberto Casati's *The Shadow Club* (New York: Knopf, 2003), translated by Abigail Asher.

The playing-card experiment is described in Jerome S. Bruner and Leo Postman's paper "On the Perception of Incongruity: A Paradigm," in the *Journal of Personality* 18 (1949), pages 206–23. It became well known after Thomas Kuhn discussed it in his *Structure of Scientific Revolutions*, 2nd ed. (Chicago: University of Chicago Press, 1970), pages 62–64.

For more on Anaximander's view of the universe see Charles Kahn's *Anaximander and the Origins of Greek Cosmology* (New York: Columbia University Press, 1960).

For a comprehensive treatment of the moon illusion see Helen Ross and Cornelis Plug, *The Mystery of the Moon Illusion: Exploring Size Perception* (Oxford: Oxford University Press, 2002). For Lieh Yü-k'ou's (列禦寇) discussion (which as a matter of fact concerns itself with the sun; the moon illusion also applies to other celestial bodies) see Édouard Claparède's "A propos de la grandeur de la lune a l'horizon" in *Archives de Psychologie* 5 (1906), page 254, as well as the German translation by Richard Wilhelm in *Liä Dsï. Das wahre Buch vom quellenden Urgrund* (Düsseldorf: Diederichs, 1974), page 107.

A VISUAL DISTORTION མིག་ཡོར།

The passage from Candrakīrti comes from his own commentary on verse 29 of chapter 6 of his *Madhyamakāvatāra*. For the Tibetan version see pages 109–10 of Louis de La Vallée Poussin's edition (St. Petersburg: Bibliotheca Buddhica IX, 1903–1913). An English paraphrase is on pages 207–8 of Geshe Kelsang Gyatso's *Ocean of Nectar* (London: Tharpa, 1995).

For the entoptic view of early nonfigurative art see J. D. Lewis-Williams and T. A. Dowson's paper "The Signs of All Times: Entoptic Phenomena in Upper Palaeolithic Art" in *Current Anthropology* 29, no. 2 (1988), pages 201–45.

The gorilla experiment is described by Daniel Simons and Christopher Chabris in their paper "Gorillas in Our Midst: Sustained Inattentional Blindness for Dynamic Events," *Perception* 28, no. 9 (1999), pages 1059–74.

For more information about Democritus see C.C.W. Taylor's *The Atomists, Leucippus and Democritus: Fragments: A Text and Translation with a Commentary* (Toronto: University of Toronto Press, 1999). For a more general discussion of atomism see Andrew Pyle's *Atomism and Its Critics: From Democritus to Newton* (Bristol: Thommes, 1997). The question of the reality of money is discussed in John Searle's *The Construction of Social Reality* (New York: Free Press, 1995).

A fascinating account of what life in a two-dimensional world could be like is given in a novel by Edwin Abbott called *Flatland*. There are various editions of this, but I recommend one by the mathematician Ian Stewart, which contains numerous enlightening notes and digressions: *The Annotated Flatland: A Romance of Many Dimensions* (Cambridge, Mass.: Perseus, 2002). A description of Hinton's cubes that the interested reader might want to construct for himself is in his *The Fourth Dimension*, (London: Swan Sonnenschein, 1906).

The beta phenomenon was first described by the German psychologist Max Wertheimer in his paper "Experimentelle Studien über das Sehen von Bewegung," *Zeitschrift für Psychologie* 61 (1912), pages 161–265. More discussion can be found in Daniel Dennett's *Consciousness Explained* (London: Penguin, 1991), as well as in Donald Hoffman's *Visual Intelligence: How We Create What We See* (New York: Norton, 1998). The reader should note that the beta phenomenon is sometimes erroneously referred to as the "phi phenomenon," which is a related but different visual illusion.

The problem of "object permanence," i.e., when two distinct perceptions are regarded as being caused by a single thing, has been investigated extensively in developmental psychology. Two now classical discussions are Jean Piaget's *Construction of Reality in the Child* (New York: Basic Books, 1955) and Elizabeth Spelke's paper "Principles of Object Perception," *Cognitive Science* 14 (1990), pages 29–56.

For a study of psychological reactions to a magic trick see E.V. Subbotskii's "Existence As a Psychological Problem: Object Permanence in Adults and Preschool Children," *International Journal of Behavioral Development* 14, no. 1 (1991), pages 67–82.

A MIRAGE སྒྱིག་རྒྱུ་

For the quotation from the *Samādhirājasūtra* see Christoph Cüpper's *The IXth chapter of the Samādhirājasūtra* (Stuttgart: Steiner, 1990), pages 96–97.

A vivid description of the realm of the hungry ghosts is given on pages 380–88 of Pabongka Rinpoche's *Liberation in the Palm of Your Hand: A Concise Discourse on the Stages of the Path to Enlightenment* (Boston: Wisdom, 1991), translated by Michael Richards.

For a clear exposition of the Yogācāra theory of the three natures based on an original text see Jay Garfield's "Vasubandhu's Treatise on the Three Natures Translated from the Tibetan Edition with a Commentary," *Asian Philosophy* 7, no. 2 (1997), pages 133–54.

For a brief introduction to phenomenalism see Alfred Ayer's essay "Phenomenalism," in his *Philosophical Essays* (London: Macmillan, 1954), pages 125–66.

The example of the lung-cancer patients comes from a paper called "On the Framing of Medical Decisions" by Barbara McNeil, Stephen Pauker, and Amos Tversky, in *Decision Making: Descriptive, Normative, and Prescriptive Interactions*, edited by David Bell, Howard Raiffa, and Amos Tversky (Cambridge: Cambridge University Press, 1988), pages 562–68. A classic account of framing is in "The Framing of Decisions and the Psychology of Choice" by Amos Tversky and Daniel Kahnemann in *Science* 211 (1981), pages 453–58. For an account incorporating framing phenomena into choice theory see Frederick Schick's *Making Choices: A Recasting of Decision Theory* (New York: Cambridge University Press, 1997).

A DREAM རྨི་ལམ་

The Tibetan text of the བི་ཏེར་ཡ་སྔོན་པོ་ is published by སྨན་རྩིས་ཤེས་རིག་སྤེན་ཛོད་, volumes 51–54 (Leh: Tashigangpa, 1973). Specific information on the Four Medical Tantras can be found in chapter 27 of *Tibetan Literature: Studies in Genre*, edited by José Ignacio Cabezón and Roger R. Jackson (Ithaca, N.Y.: Snow Lion, 1995). For a general introduction to Tibetan medicine the interested reader may want to consult Terry Clifford's *Tibetan Buddhist Medicine and Psychiatry* (York Beach Weiser, 1984), and *Fundamentals of Tibetan Medicine: According to the Rgyud-bzhi* (Dharamsala: Tibetan Medical Centre, 1981), translated and edited by T. J. Tsarong. A beautiful two-volume set with reproductions of the medical paintings has been published as *Tibetan Medical Paintings* (New York: Abrams, 1992), edited by Yuri Parfionovitch, Gyurme Dorje, and Fernand Meyer.

For more information on the Six Yogas of Nāropa the reader might want to consult the following three texts, which are also the source of the quotations: the sixteenth-century ཆོས་དྲུག་བསྡུས་པའི་ཟིན་བྲིས་ by Pema Karpo (པད་མ་དཀར་པོ་), translated as book 3 of W.Y. Evans-Wentz's *Tibetan Yoga and Secret Doctrines*, 2nd ed. (Oxford: Oxford University Press, 1958); the twelfth-century མཁས་གྲུབ་ཀུན་གྱི་གཙུག་རྒྱན་པཎ་ཆེན་ནཱ་རོ་པའི་རྣམ་པར་ཐར་པ་ཨོཚར་སྣང་ཧྲུང་ by Lhatsun Rinchen Namgyal (ལྷ་བཙུན་རིན་ཆེན་རྣམ་རྒྱལ་), translated by Herbert V. Guenther in *The Life and Teachings of Naropa* (Oxford: Oxford University Press, 1963); and Tsong kha pa's (1357–1419) ཟབ་ལམ་ནཱ་རོའི་ཆོས་དྲུག་གི་སྒོ་ནས་འཁྲིད་པའི་རིམ་པ་ཡིད་ཆེས་གསུམ་ལྡན་, a commentary on the Six Yogas, translated by Glenn H. Mullin as *The Six Yogas of Naropa* (Ithaca, N.Y.: Snow Lion, 2005). All three are widely available.

Information about the empirical studies of *tummo* can be found in Herbert Benson's "Body Temperature Changes during the Practice of gTum-mo Yoga," *Nature* 295 (1982), 234–36.

There are various modern editions of Saint-Denys's book. A partial English translation by Nicholas Fry was published under the title *Dreams and How to Guide Them* (London: Duckworth, 1982). The passages quoted can be found on page 57.

Keith Hearne's experiments involving the first recorded signals from a lucid dream are described in his unpublished doctoral dissertation *Lucid Dreams: An Electrophysiological and Psychological Study* (Liverpool: University of Liverpool, 1978). Further fascinating empirical research into lucid dreaming has been carried out by Stephen LaBerge at Stanford University. A good overview (though very much in the style of a how-to manual) is his *Exploring the World of Lucid Dreaming*, coauthored with Howard Rheingold (New York: Ballantine, 1990). LaBerge relates Tibetan dream practices to contemporary findings in his paper "Lucid Dreaming and the Yoga of the Dream State: A Psychophysiological Perspective," in *Buddhism and Science: Breaking New Ground*, edited by B. Alan Wallace (New York: Columbia University Press, 2003), pages 233–58.

More information about the estimation of time in dreams can be found in La Berge's *Lucid Dreaming* (Los Angeles: Tarcher, 1985).

The quotation concerning brain activity during sleep is from William Dement's *Some Must Watch, While Some Must Sleep* (Stanford: Stanford Alumni Association, 1972), page 49.

The question "who is dreaming?" is also addressed in Thomas Metzinger, *The Ego Tunnel: The Science of the Mind and the Myth of the Self* (New York: Basic Books, 2009), page 135.

A fascinating if not always very systematic account of the place of dreams in Indian culture is given by Wendy Doniger O'Flaherty in her *Dreams, Illusion, and Other Realities* (Chicago: University of Chicago Press, 1984).

AN ECHO སྒྲ་བརྙན་

More information on Golconda Fort can be found in Shehbaz Safrani's *Golconda and Hyderabad* (Bombay: Marg Publications, 1992).

The passages from the *Mahāprajñāpāramitāśāstra* are on pages 368–69 of Etienne Lamotte's translation *Le traité de la grande vertu de sagesse* (Louvain: Bureaux du Muséon, 1944). For a Buddhist meditational exercise on echoes that proceeds in a similar fashion see Garma C. C. Chang's translation, *Teachings of Tibetan Yoga* (Hyde Park, N.Y.: University Books, 1963), page 83.

A stationary conception of sounds is defended in Casey O'Callaghan's paper "Echoes," *The Monist* 90 (2007), pages 403–14. A more technical discussion is in Jens Blauert's *Spatial Hearing: The Psychophysics of Human Sound Localization* (Cambridge, Mass.: MIT Press, 1997). For a more general philosophical treatment see Roberto Casati and Jérôme Dokic, *La philosophie du son* (Nîmes: Éditions Jacqueline Chambon, 1994).

The theory of the different locations for the production of speech and the corresponding classification of sounds is treated in detail in Indian phonetics. See W. S. Allen's *Phonetics in Ancient India* (London: Oxford University Press, 1953), in particular pages 23–24.

Joseph Weizenbaum gives a short technical description of the program in "ELIZA—A Computer Program for the Study of Natural Language Communication between Man and Machine," *Communications of the Association for Computing Machinery (ACM)* 9, no. 1 (1966), pages 36–45. An online version of Weizenbaum's original ELIZA can be found at www.chayden.net/eliza/Eliza.html. For some reflection caused by reactions to ELIZA see his *Computer Power and Human Reason: From Judgment to Calculation* (San Francisco: W. H. Freeman, 1976).

More information about Daniel Dennett's notion of the "intentional stance" can be found in his book of the same title (Cambridge, Mass.: MIT Press, 1987). At this point I should also recommend what is probably the most mind-bending book on artificial intelligence ever written, Douglas Hofstadter's *Gödel, Escher, Bach: An Eternal Golden Braid* (New York: Basic Books, 1979). It will particularly appeal to readers who, like its author, are not interested in computers.

THE CITY OF GANDHARVAS དྲི་ཟའི་གྲོང་ཁྱེར་

The passage from the *Mahāprajñāpāramitāśāstra* is on page 369 of Etienne Lamotte's translation *Le traité de la grande vertu de sagesse* (Louvain: Bureaux du Muséon, 1944). For some mythological information on the Gandharvas see Benjamin Walker's *Hindu World: An Encyclopedic Survey of Hinduism* (New York: Praeger, 1968), pages 370–71. For the role of the Gandharva Viśvāvasu in the Hindu marriage rites see the *R̥g Veda* 10.85.21–22, 40–41. An accessible translation is in Wendy Doniger O'Flaherty's *The Rig Veda: An Anthology* (London: Penguin, 1981), pages 269–71.

Some of the many letters written to Sherlock Holmes are collected in Richard Lancelyn Green's *Letters to Sherlock Holmes* (London: Penguin, 1986). For Watson's wandering wound see the discussion in *The New Annotated Sherlock Holmes,* edited by Leslie S. Klinger (New York: Norton, 2006), pages 7–14.

A fascinating encyclopedia of fictional places is Alberto Manguel and Gianni Guadalupi's *Dictionary of Imaginary Places*, rev. ed. (New York: Harcourt Brace, 2000). Two popular yet well-informed books on Tibetan hidden lands are Edwin Bernbaum's *The Way to Shambhala: A Search for the Mythical Kingdom beyond the Himalayas* (Boston: Shambhala, 2001; the excerpt from the guidebook to Shambhala quoted by me is on pages 192–93) and Ian Baker's *The Heart of the World: A Journey to the Last Secret Place* (New York: Penguin, 2004). For a more scholarly discussion of guidebooks to Shambhala the reader might want to consult chapter 29 of *Tibetan Literature: Studies in Genre*, edited by José Ignacio Cabezón and Roger R. Jackson (Ithaca, N.Y.: Snow Lion, 1996). It is interesting to note that Sherlock Holmes reached Shambhala during his mysterious stay in Tibet. The story of his travels is very well described in Jamyang Norbu's *The Mandala of Sherlock Holmes* (New Delhi: HarperCollins, 1999).

Vasubandhu's discussion of the guardians of hell is in verses 4–6 of his *Viṃśatikā Vijñaptimātratāsiddhi*. See part 2 of Fernando Tola and Carmen Dragonetti's *Being as Consciousness: Yogācāra Philosophy of Buddhism* (Delhi: Motilal Banarsidass, 2004), pages 82–88 and 136–39. For a take on the idea of reality as fiction slightly different from the one presented here see Charles Crittenden's paper "Everyday Reality as Fiction—A Mādhyamika Interpretation" in the *Journal of Indian Philosophy* 9, no. 4 (1981), pages 323–33. For a related discussion see the section "The Construction of Nonreality" in Stephan Beyer's *Magic and Ritual in Tibet: The Cult of Tara* (Delhi: Motilal Banarsidass, 1998), pages 92–108.

For Vasubandhu's account of the Gandharva in his *Abhidharmakośabhāṣya* see the second volume of Leo M. Pruden's English translation of La Vallée Poussin's French translation (Berkeley, Calif.: Asian Humanities Press, 1988), pages 386–91.

The reader interested in the Tibetan description of the intermediate state should consult *The Tibetan Book of the Dead: First Complete Translation*, edited by Graham Coleman with Thupten Jinpa (London: Penguin, 2006). For the relevant passage of the *Śālistambhasūtra* see section 36 of N. Ross Reat's edition and translation in his *The Śālistambhasūtra: Tibetan Original, Sanskrit Reconstruction, English Translation, Critical Notes (Including Pāli Parallels, Chinese Version and Ancient Tibetan Fragments)* (Delhi: Motilal Banarsidass, 1993), page 64.

The quotation from Daniel Dennett is from his *Consciousness Explained* (London: Penguin, 1991), page 418. For a more detailed discussion of the view of the self as a fictional character see his "The Self as the Center of Narrative Gravity," in *Self and Consciousness: Multiple Perspectives*, edited by Frank Kessel, Pamela Cole, and Dale Johnson (Hillsdale, N.J.: Erlbaum, 1992), pages 105–11.

AN OPTICAL ILLUSION མིག་འཕྲུལ་

For the passage from the *Laṅkāvatārasūtra* see the translation by Daisetz Teitaro Suzuki (London: Routledge, 1932), pages 90–92. Further uses of the example of the wheel of fire in Buddhist philosophical discussion are listed in part 2 of Hajime Nakamura's *History of Early Vedānta Philosophy*, translated by Trevor Leggett (Delhi: Motilal Banarsidass, 2004), pages 256 and 358.

For discussion of flicker perception and the temporal resolution of the human eye see Ralph Norman Haber and Maurice Hershenson, *The Psychology of Visual Perception* (New York: Holt, Rinehart and Winston, 1973), pages 140–45. It has been suggested that there is a correlation between the degree of temporal resolution and the brain's alpha-rhythm. See Francisco Varela, Alfredo Toro, E. Roy John, and Eric L. Schwartt, "Perceptual Framing and Cortical Alpha-rhythm," *Neuropsychologia* 19, no. 5 (1981), pages 675–86, for some discussion.

The quotation from Isaac Newton can be found on page 347 of his *Opticks, or, A Treatise of the Reflections, Refractions, Inflections & Colours of Light*, reprint of the 4th ed. from 1730 (New York: Dover, 1952).

Why our perception of films should not be understood in terms of the notion of persistence of vision is explained in Joseph and Barbara Anderson's "The Myth of Persistence of Vision Revisited," *Journal of Film and Video* 45, no. 1 (1993), pages 3–12.

A detailed discussion of the idea of "filling in" is in the paper "Finding Out About Filling In: A Guide to Perceptual Completion for Visual Science and the Philosophy of Perception," by Luiz Pessoa, Evan Thompson, and Alva Noë, *Behavioral and Brain Sciences* 21, no. 6 (1998), pages 723–48, 796–802.

A brief presentation of the Abhidharma theory of moments is on pages 134–44 of Edward Conze's *Buddhist Thought in India* (Ann Arbor: University of Michigan Press, 1967). I follow Conze in assuming that there are seventy-five moments to a second. However, other accounts of the length of a moment can be found in Buddhist literature as well.

For a comprehensive discussion of the theory of moments see Alexander von Rospatt's *The Buddhist Doctrine of Momentariness: A Survey of the Origins and Early Phase of this Doctrine up to Vasubandhu* (Stuttgart: Steiner, 1995).

Later Buddhist criticism of the Abhidharma theory of moments is discussed in chapter 11 of Āryadeva's *Catuḥśataka*. An accessible English edition with commentary by Geshe Sonam Rinchen is *Yogic Deeds of Bodhisattvas*, translated and edited by Ruth Sonam (Ithaca, N.Y.: Snow Lion, 1994), pages 227–38.

For psychological studies on the perception of the duration of the present see the entry on "time perception" in the *Encyclopedia of Neuroscience*, edited by George Adelman and Barry Smith, 2nd ed. (Amsterdam: Elsevier, 1999), pages 2047–48, as well as chapters 2 to 9 of Ernst Pöppel's *Mind Works: Time and Conscious Experience*, translated by Tom Artin (Boston: Harcourt Brace Jovanovich, 1988).

A more detailed exposition of the Madhyamaka criticism of the Abhidharma view is in Mark Siderits's paper "Causation and Emptiness in Early Madhyamaka," *Journal of Indian Philosophy* 32, no. 4 (2004), pages 393–419.

RAINBOWS འཇའ་ཚོན་

A comprehensive treatment of various aspects of rainbows can be found in Carl B. Boyer's *The Rainbow: From Myth to Mathematics*, rev. ed. (Princeton, N.J.: Princeton

University Press, 1987). More references to a variety of mythological views of rainbows in different cultures are in Mircea Eliade's *Shamanism*, translated by Willard Trask (London: Arkana, 1989), pages 131–35.

The most well-known translation of Milarepa's biography is still that of W. Y. Evans-Wentz, *Tibet's Great Yogi, Milarepa* (London: Oxford University Press, 1928), which has been reprinted in various editions. It is nowadays more interesting on historical grounds than on those of linguistic accuracy. Evans-Wentz's translation of the passage given is on pages 286–87. A more recent translation, by Lobsang P. Lhalungpa, was published as *The Life of Milarepa* in 1977 (New York: Dutton). Readers interested in the Tibetan text should consult མི་ལ་རས་པའི་རྣམ་ཐར་, edited by Jan Willem de Jong ('s Gravenhage: Mouton, 1959). The relevant section is to be found on pages 192, lines 12–14 and 21–23.

For a brief account of the early Tibetan kings and the rainbow cord see Giuseppe Tucci, *Tibetan Painted Scrolls* (Rome: Libreria dello Stato, 1949), pages 733–34. Readers interested in more historical detail might want to look at Erik Haarh's *The Yar-luṅ Dynasty* (Copenhagen: Gad, 1969).

A variety of historical accounts of Buddhist masters dissolving into rainbow light can be found in Tulku Thondup's *Masters of Meditation and Miracles*, edited by Harold Talbott (Boston: Shambala, 1996). For a description of contemporary examples see *The Crystal and the Way of Light: Sutra, Tantra, and Dzogchen: The Teachings of Namkhai Norbu*, edited by John Shane (London: Routledge & Kegan Paul, 1986), as well as *Graceful Exits: How Great Beings Die: Death Stories of Hindu, Tibetan Buddhist, and Zen Masters*, edited by Sushila Blackman (Boston: Shambhala, 2005), pages 46–47. For an interesting interpretation of the rainbow body as the brain's self-model see Thomas Metzinger, *The Ego Tunnel: The Sciences of the Mind and the Myth of the Self* (New York: Basic Books, 2009), page 86.

LIGHTNING གློག

Further details of the life of Tsangpa Gyare can be found in the *Blue Annals*, translated by George Roerich (Delhi: Motilal Banarsidass, 1976), 664–70. For information about Namdruk Monastery see Keith Dowman's *The Power-Places of Central Tibet* (London: Routledge & Kegan Paul, 1988), page 136. A description of the place of the dragon in Tibetan mythology is on pages 63–65 of Robert Beer's *Encyclopedia of Tibetan Symbols and Motifs* (Boston: Shambhak, 1999).

Wundt's investigations of temporal illusions are described in the third volume of his *Grundzüge der physiologischen Psychologie*, 5th ed. (Leipzig: Engelmann, 1902–1903), pages 53–86. A summary can be found in the chapter 11 of Willam James's *The Principles of Psychology* (New York: Henry Holt, 1890).

An account of Libet's experiments can be found in his paper "The Experimental Evidence for Subjective Referral of a Sensory Experience Backwards in Time," in *Philosophy of Science* 48, no. 2 (1981), pages 182–97. Karl Popper and John Eccles argue on page 376 of *The Self and Its Brain* (New York: Springer, 1977) that Libet's experiments raise problems for equating the mind with what the brain does. An extended discussion of the philosophical implications of Libet's results is given in chapters 5 and 6 of Daniel Dennett's *Consciousness Explained* (London: Penguin, 1991).

WATER BUBBLES ཆུ་བུར་

The passage from the *Phena Sutta* comes from Bhikkhu Bodhi's *The Connected Discourses of the Buddha: A New Translation of the Saṃyutta Nikāya*, (Boston: Pali Text Society and Wisdom Publications, 2001), page 951. I have translated *rūpa* as "matter" instead of the more familiar "form."

More information on the nature and widespread occurrence of all sorts of foam can be found in Sidney Perkowitz's *Universal Foam: Explaining the Science of Nature's Most Mysterious Substance* (New York: Anchor, 2000). In his paper "Particles Do Not Exist" P.C.W. Davies argues against regarding particles as anything more real than an idealized model in a very limited context; in *Quantum Theory of Gravity*, edited by Steven Christensen (Bristol: Hilger, 1984), pages 66–77. A popular account of string theory is provided by Brian Greene in his *Elegant Universe* (New York: Vintage, 2000).

For a very clear discussion of the question whether strings (or their theoretical competitors) are likely to constitute the most basic layer of reality see Jonathan Schaffer, "Is There a Fundamental Level? *Noûs* 37, no. 7 (2003), pages 498–517.

The quotation from Vasubandhu comes from verse 12 of his *Viṃśatikā Vijñaptimātratāsiddhi*. An accessible edition of the Sanskrit text, together with a translation and commentary, can be found in part 2 of Fernando Tola and Carmen Dragonetti's *Being as Consciousness: Yogācāra Philosophy of Buddhism* (Delhi: Motilal Banarsidass, 2004), pages 53–186. For more discussion of Vasubandhu's argument the interested reader might want to consult Matthew Kapstein's "Mereological Considerations in Vasubandhu's 'Proof of Idealism'" in his *Reason's Traces* (Boston: Wisdom Publications, 2001), pages 181–204.

A discussion of the nature of holes can be found in a dialogue of the same title, by David and Stephanie Lewis, reprinted in volume 1 of the former's *Philosophical Papers* (New York: Oxford University Press, 1983), pages 3–9. In this conversation between two characters called Argle and Bargle, Argle defends the materialist view of holes as inner hole linings. A book-length treatment of philosophical issues that holes generate is in *Holes and Other Superficialities* by Roberto Casati and Achille Varzi (Cambridge, Mass.: MIT Press, 1994).

Details on the Hedonistic Calculus may be found in chapter 4 of Jeremy Bentham's *An Introduction to the Principles of Morals and Legislation* (London: Payne, 1789).

The "hedonic treadmill" is analyzed in Philip Brickman and Donald Campbell's "Hedonic Relativism and Planning the Good Society," in *Adaptation–level Theory: A Symposium*, edited by M. H. Apley (New York: Academic Press, 1971), pages 287–302.

The fruit fly experiment is described in Hiromi Tanimoto, Martin Heisenberg, and Bertram Gerber, "Experimental Psychology: Event Timing Turns Punishment to Reward," *Nature* 430, no. 7003 (2004), page 983.

For the quotation from Tsong kha pa see volume 1 of his *Great Treatise on the Stages of the Path to Enlightenment*, translated by the Lamrim Translation Committee (Ithaca, N.Y.: Snow Lion, 2000), page 296.

A REFLECTION IN A MIRROR མེ་ལོང་ནང་གི་གཟུགས་བརྙན་

A good overview of the example of a reflection in a mirror in a variety of Buddhist contexts is Alex Wayman's paper "The Mirror as a Pan-Buddhist Metaphor-simile," *History of Religions* 13, no. 4 (1974), pages 251–69.

The ritual of consecration for a Tibetan *thangka* is described in volume 1 of Giuseppe Tucci's monumental *Tibetan Painted Scrolls* (Rome: Libreria dello Stato, 1949), beginning on page 308.

The description of the ritual of bathing the image is from Stephan Beyer's *Magic and Ritual in Tibet: The Cult of Tara* (Delhi: Motilal Banarsidass, 1998), pages 336–37.

On pages 162–63 of his interesting paper "Structure and Meaning of the Rite Called Bath of the Buddha According to Tibetan and Chinese Sources," *Studia Serica Bernhard Karlgren Dedicata*, edited by Søren Egerod and Elso Glahn (Copenhagen: Munksgaard, 1959), pages 159–71, Ferdinand Lessing mentions an interesting variety of the performance of the bathing ritual where the water is poured into a basin located between the image and the mirror, as if to purify the reflected rays of light:

> He [that is the officiating priest] places the basin and the flask between the image and the mirror. Then he begins to chant the sixty stanzas of the ritual. At certain intervals he pours water from the flask into the basin, holding the flask so that the rays imagined as issuing from the image pass through the water to the mirror, from which they are reflected back to the flask. Thereupon the officiant dabs the mirror at four places with pieces of cloth. This act is repeated a number of times during the main part of the ceremony. At the end of the liturgy the lama pours the water back into the flask. If the rite is performed at the request of a layman, the lama will pour a few drops into the palm of the bystanders, who taste it imagining that thus the essence of the Buddha fills their bodies and appears changed on their heads into the evoked deity, thus making them co-substantial with him.

A translation of བགྲའ་ཤེས་རྣམ་རྒྱལ་'s ནརོ་ཆོས་དྲུག་གི་གཀ་འདི་ is given in Garma C. C. Chang's *Teachings of Tibetan Yoga* (Hyde Park, N.Y.: University Books, 1963). Translations of the passages quoted are on pages 82–84.

Martin Gardner, in his *New Ambidextrous Universe: Symmetry and Asymmetry from Mirror Reflections to Superstrings*, 3rd ed. (Mineola, N.Y.: Dover, 2005), pages 19–22, offers an account of the question of why mirrors seem to reverse left and right but not up and down similar to the one in terms of "mental rotation" suggested by me. Richard Gregory, in his *Mirrors in Mind* (Oxford: Oxford University Press, 1996), pages 84–106, disagrees. Further accounts can be found in two papers with very similar titles. The first, by Ned Block, is called "Why Do Mirrors Reverse Right/Left but Not Up/Down?" and was published in the *Journal of Philosophy* 71 (1974), pages 259–77. The other one, called "Why Do Mirrors Reverse Left/Right and Not Up/Down?" introduces the set of directional terms based on the notion of "cordial." It was written by Nicholas Denyer and came out in *Philosophy* 69, no. 268 (1994), pages 205–10. On the whole it seems fair to say that a consensus on how to explain the illusion has not emerged yet.

V.S. Ramachandran's story about the cup is on page 43 of his *Phantoms in the Brain: Probing the Mysteries of the Human Mind* (New York: William Morrow, 1998). The experiment with the mirror box is described in the paper "Touching the Phantom Limb" by V.S. Ramachandran, D. C. Rogers-Ramachandran, and S. Cobb, *Nature* 377, no. 6549 (1995), pages 489–90.

REVIEW OF "TWELVE
EXAMPLES OF ILLUSION"

Journal of Indo-Tibetan Studies 27, no. 3

The last couple of years have seen a variety of publications attempting to connect Tibetan Buddhism with the natural sciences. Matthieu Ricard, a former student of the French biologist Jacques Monod and a Buddhist monk, brought out a series of dialogues between himself and the Vietnamese astronomer Trịnh Xuân Thuận under the title *The Quantum and the Lotus*,[52] which explore presumed relations between Tibetan Buddhist philosophy and present-day physics. Some years before that, Allan B. Wallace, a former Buddhist monk, published *Choosing Reality*,[53] an investigation of the implications of Buddhist thought for the philosophy of science. Even the Dalai Lama himself sometimes engages in exchanges with Western scientists, as the publications arising from the "Mind and Life" conferences testify.[54]

One might well wonder why a Tibetan contemplative tradition going back 1,300 years that is based in turn on an Indian contemplative tradition going back another 1,200 years should be asked to enter into a meaningful exchange with present-day evidence-based natural science. Claims that some of the latter's insights (usually of a highly theoretical and often speculative nature, such as that of the role of the observer in quantum physics, or the absence of a "Cartesian theater" in the brain) have somehow been anticipated by the former certainly have strange intellectual bedfellows—the reviewer is reminded of the "Baghdad battery,"[55] the "Egyptian light-bulb" supposedly depicted at the temple of Hathor at Dendera,[56] and ancient Indian aeronautics.[57]

While such backward projections are not to be taken seriously, there might be a point in arguing that an ancient and alien system of thought can be *explained* using concepts from present-day science familiar to the contemporary reader, without

---

52. New York: Crown, 2001. It was originally published in French as *L'infini dans la paume de la main* (Paris: Fayard, 2000).

53. Boston: New Science Library, 1989.

54. For the results of the first of these, held in Dharamsala in 1987, see *Gentle Bridges: Conversations with the Dalai Lama on the Sciences of the Mind,* edited by Jeremy Hayward and Francisco Varela (Boston: Shambhala, 1992).

55. Gerhard Eggert, "The Enigmatic 'Battery of Baghdad,'" *Skeptical Inquirer* 20, no. 3 (1996), pages 31–34.

56. Peter Krassa and Reinhard Habeck, *Das Licht der Pharaonen* (Munich: Herbig, 1996).

57. Dileep Kumar Kanjilal, *Vimāna in Ancient India* (Calcutta: Sanskrit Pustak Bhandar, 1985).

presupposing that these concepts have already been anticipated by the ancients. Our current knowledge of anatomy can help to explain why Stone Age men carried out trepanations, but this does not imply that they had a clear conception of intracranial pressure.

This kind of explanation may be what Westerhoff is trying to provide us with. He dresses up his account as a commentary on a passage from dKon mchog 'jigs med dbang po's "Tibetan Encyclopaedia" *mDo rgyud bstan bcos du ma nas 'byung ba'i chos kyi rnam grangs shes ldan yid kyi dga' ston.* But this is wrong in at least two respects. First of all the text is no "encyclopedia" at all but rather a pocket-sized specialized dictionary (my own paperback copy of this text runs to less than 180 pages). It was aimed at a reader of Tibetan scholastic literature who might come across a reference to something like the "six excretions" and not know what this was.[58] He would then be able to look this up among other "sets of six things." But dKon mchog 'jigs med dbang po does not give any explanation of the terms he lists. We are unable to look up the *meaning* of any of the terms given, and therefore this text is no encyclopedia. A cynic might want to say that Westerhoff takes the notorious verbosity of Indian and Tibetan scholastic commentators to new heights by offering a two-hundred-page commentary on twelve words.[59] This would not be entirely fair, but only because Westerhoff's book is no commentary.

Throughout the text Westerhoff operates under the counterfactual assumption (dare I say "illusion"?) that the Indian and Tibetan writers who employed the twelve examples of illusion had twelve clear and distinctly delineated aspects of illusion in mind that these examples were supposed to illustrate. The implausibility of this assumption is evident from the fact (which Westerhoff himself notes) that the list of twelve presented by dKon mchog 'jigs med dbang po is only one of many differing lists found in the literature. There is simply no textual evidence that a single Indian or Tibetan writer thought that illusions had twelve different characteristics, and that these were instantiated by the twelve examples. The examples were given to illustrate how the author (and the tradition he represented) claimed that the notion of an illusion was to be understood. There was no assumption that, for example, an illusory mirage operated in any philosophically interesting way differently from an illusory magical projection. The textual sources Westerhoff himself presents as support of his attempt to connect the twelve examples with twelve different aspects of illusion are therefore precisely his own ideas projected into the material and are no more present in the textual material than water is in a mirage. Rather than seeing Westerhoff's text as a commentary it is more accurate to regard it as a description of the associations that the examples of illusions triggered in his own mind, somewhat embellished by Indian and Tibetan textual sources.

Westerhoff's philosophical discussion has the disconcerting habit of frequently breaking off when the matter gets interesting. To a certain extent this may be due to the fact that

---

58. For the record (page 72): feces, urine, eye mucus, ear wax, saliva, and snot.

59. A contemporary Tibetologist observes that the "tedium" of a baroque architecture of sections, sub-sections, sub-sub-sections, and so on that the seventeenth-century Tibetan rGyal tshab rje superimposes on the second-century Indian Nāgārjuna's *Ratnāvalī* is "mitigated by appreciating the creative task of fabricating such a detailed outline" (Jeffrey Hopkins, *Buddhist Advice for Living and Liberation: Nāgārjuna's Precious Garland* [Ithaca, N.Y.: Snow Lion, 1998], page 94). Whether similarly mitigating circumstances are present in the case of Westerhoff's *opus* I leave for others to decide.

the book is written for a general reader, and not a specialized audience of philosophers. Nevertheless I cannot help thinking that sometimes having fewer pictures and more arguments would have done the book a favor.

The arguments we do find occasionally lead to bizarre consequences. On page 113 Westerhoff argues that our decision to regard some phenomenon as an intentional agent has to be based on pragmatic (read "utilitarian") considerations, and not on the nature of the phenomenon. So it seems to be the case that if our utilitarian cost-benefit analysis tells us that it is not feasible to consider patients in a permanent vegetative state as intentional agents, whereas some very sophisticated future computers should be regarded in this way, switching off the power for the life support of the former is morally permissible, whereas pulling the plug on the latter is not. This consequence strikes me as sufficiently nonsensical to function as a *reductio ad absurdum* of the argument Westerhoff presents.

I also take issue with Westerhoff's conception of substance, given on page 51, as something that does not depend on anything else. If we define it in this way we end up either as Democritean atomists or as Spinoza-style monists. It is interesting to note that an individual self would not be a substance in either case: in the first it would be nothing but an epiphenomenal property of random interactions between atoms, in the second case it could only be a property of the Great One.

But this alternative does not present itself to us since Westerhoff's definition of substance is not satisfactory. If we define substance rather as something that cannot be created or destroyed we obtain a conception that actually lets us know what substances there are, and does so on a naturalistic basis: charge will be a substance in electrodynamics, mass will be one in classical mechanics.

The advantage of this definition is that it shows substance to be theory-dependent. If we switch to relativistic mechanics, mass ceases to be a substance and becomes simply a particular manifestation of the new substance, namely energy. According to this account Westerhoff's insubstantial holes might turn out to be substances after all, given the right theoretical framework (consider bubbles in a finite amount of incompressible liquid). A large section of the humanities will regard the self as a substance, even though it will not be a substance for cognitive science.

The crunch now is the question of whether some things are substances relative to *any* theory. It is easy to see that this is not the case. Consider epidemiology. It is conceivable that all populations of living beings die out. The extinction of all life is a possibility within the framework of epidemiological theory, while, for example, a world without material substances would be no possibility in the theoretical framework of physics. Since *all* the entities epidemiology deals with could cease to exist none of them are substances relative to that theory. But if there are "substanceless" theories of this kind there cannot be anything that is a substance relative to any theory.

But the defender of substances might not have to despair yet. He could try to locate the substantial existents in the preconditions of forming any theory (both representational systems like language and the observer seem to be plausible candidates here). These would not be substances *relative to a theory*, since we could not make any statements about whether they can be created or destroyed—after all we have to assume them in order to make any theoretical statements at all. These substances have to be there, but this is about everything we could ever know about them.

So we are faced with the choice: We can either regard substance as a transcendental reality about which very little can be said, or as an illusory unreality about which we can say many things. Whether *this* choice is a real choice or merely an illusory one I leave for the reader to decide.[60]

JAMPA LODRÖ
King's Hall, Cambridge

---

60. The *Journal of Indo-Tibetan Studies* does not exist. The preceding pages have been written by the author of this book.

CREDITS

Page 4   Gung-thang Bstan-pa'i-sgron-me: Kun mkhyen 'Jam-dbyangs-bzhad-pa sku phreng gnyis pa rje 'Jigs-med-dbang-po'i rnam thar, Lan-chou, 1990.

Page 5   *Collected Works of Könchog Jigme Wangpo* (New Delhi, 1971).

Page 6   Nepalese woodblock print, author's collection.

Page 10   Map by Jan Westerhoff.

Page 11   Ananda Coomaraswamy: *La sculpture de Bharhut* (Paris:Vanoest, 1956), 53–54.

Page 12   Vendla von Langenn: Bettler, Heilige und Maharajas (Stuttgart: Deutsche Verlags-Anstalt, 1949).

Page 13   Collection of Shelley and Donald Rubin. Himalayan Art Resources (www.himalayanart.org).

Page 14   Wilhelm Filchner: *Das Kloster Kumbum in Tibet* (Berlin: ES Mittler und Sohn, 1906).

Page 15   Françoise Borin, *Le Tibet d' Alexandra David-Neél* (Paris: Plon, 1979).

Page 19   Diagram by Jan Westerhoff.

Page 24   Nepalese woodblock print, author's collection.

Page 24   Photograph of the Wheel of Life © Elizabeth Napper and Daniel E. Perdue, from a *thangka* in the possession of Daniel E. Perdue.

Page 25   Nepalese woodblock print, author's collection.

Page 25   Detail from Nepalese woodblock print.

Page 25   Detail from Nepalese woodblock print, author's collection.

Page 26   Print by Ohara Koson. Photo courtesy of the Caroline Black Print Collection, Connecticut College, New London.

Page 27   Jules Cashford: *Im Bann des Mondes* (Egmont, 2003).

Page 30   Robert Beer: *The Encyclopedia of Tibetan Symbols and Motifs* (Serindia, 2004).

Page 32   Galileo Galilei: *Sidereus Nuncius* (Venice, 1610).

Page 33   Photograph by Jan Westerhoff.

Page 34   http://astronomy.swim.edu.

Page 36   Photographs by Mila Zinkova.

Page 38   With permission of Richard Gregory.

Page 42   Nepalese woodblock print, author's collection.

Page 42   Diagram by Jan Westerhoff.

Page 44   D.J. Simons and C. F. Chabris, "Gorillas in Our Midst: Sustained Inattentional Blindness for Dynamic Events," *Perception* 28 (1999), 1059–74.

Page 46   Image courtesy E. F. Redish, Physicists on the Money (www.physics.umd.edu/~redish/Money).

Page 51   Charles Howard Hinton: *The Fourth Dimension* (London: Sonnenschein, 1904).

Page 57   With permission of the Royal Ontario Museum © ROM.

Page 59   Photograph courtesy of Mila Zinkova.

Page 60   Edi Lanners, *Illusions* (New York: Henry Holt, 1977).

Page 61   Nepalese woodblock print, author's collection.

Page 61   Nepalese woodblock print, author's collection.

Page 62   Photograph by Augusto Gansser.

Page 70   Yuri Parfionovitch, Gyurme Dorje, and Fernand Meyer, eds., *Tibetan Medical Paintings* (New York: Abrams, 1992).

Page 71   Yuri Parfionovitch, Gyurme Dorje, and Fernand Meyer, eds., *Tibetan Medical Paintings* (New York: Abrams, 1992).

Page 71   Yuri Parfionovitch, Gyurme Dorje, and Fernand Meyer, eds., *Tibetan Medical Paintings* (New York: Abrams, 1992).

Page 72   Photograph © 2010 Museum of Fine Arts, Boston.

Page 73   © Rubin Museum of Art/Art Resource, New York.

Page 76   Hervey de Saint-Denys, *Les rêves et les moyens de les diriger: observations pratiques* (Paris, 1867).

Page 78   Stephen LaBerge, "Lucid Dreaming: Evidence and Methodology," *Behavioral and Brain Sciences* 23, no. 6, 962–63.

Page 80   Photograph by Jan Westerhoff.

Page 81   Photograph by Jan Westerhoff.

Page 83   Photograph by Jan Westerhoff.

Page 86   © Rubin Museum of Art/Art Resource, New York.

Page 96   © Rubin Museum of Art/Art Resource, New York.

Page 97   © The Sherlock Holmes Museum, 221b Baker Street, London, England. www.sherlock-holmes.co.uk.

Page 100   Book cover, 37th impression of *Lost Horizon* by James Hilton (New York: Pocket Books, 1945).

Page 101   © Rubin Museum of Art/Art Resource, New York.

Page 102   © Rubin Museum of Art/Art Resource, New York.

Page 103   With permission of the Royal Ontario Museum © ROM.

Page 106   © Rubin Museum of Art/Art Resource, New York.

Page 108   Photograph by Thomas Laird.

Page 111   Edi Lanners, *Illusions* (New York: Henry Holt, 1977).

Page 111   Image courtesy of Andrew Davidhazy.

Page 112   Image courtesy of Andrew Davidhazy.

Page 115   Diagram by Jan Westerhoff.

Page 119   Schøyen Collection.

Page 123   Hiroki Fujita, *Chibetto Bukkyo Bijutsu* (Fujita Hiroki Shashinshu, Hakusuisha, 1984).

Page 125   Ken Holmes, *Karmapa* (Forres: Altea Publishing, 1995).

Page 125   Rober Beer, *The Encyclopedia of Tibetan Symbols and Motifs* (Serindia, 2004).

Page 126   © Rubin Museum of Art/Art Resource, New York.

Page 127   © Rubin Museum of Art/Art Resource, New York.

Page 137   Photograph by Jan Westerhoff.

Page 138   © Rubin Museum of Art/Art Resource, New York.

Page 139   E. Zimmermann, *Psychologische und physiologische apparate* (Leipzig: Heine, 1928).

Page 152   © Rubin Museum of Art/Art Resource, New York.

Page 157   Photograph by Jan Westerhoff.

Page 162   © Rubin Museum of Art/Art Resource, New York.

Page 162   G. W. Essen collection.

Page 165   Photograph by Jan Westerhoff.

Page 165   Photograph by Jan Westerhoff.

INDEX